D11172439

NO FEAR SHAKESPEARE

NO FEAR SHAKESPEARE

Hamlet

Julius Caesar

King Lear

Macbeth

The Merchant of Venice

A Midsummer Night's Dream

Othello

Romeo and Juliet

The Tempest

Twelfth Night

NO FEAR SHAKESPEARE

JULIUS CAESAR

Edited by
John Crowther

SPARK
NOTES

EDITORIAL DIRECTOR: Justin Kestler

EXECUTIVE EDITOR: Ben Florman

DIRECTOR OF TECHNOLOGY: Tammy Hepps

SERIES EDITOR: John Crowther

CONTRIBUTING EDITORS: Anna Medvedovsky, Laura Heffernan, Matt Blanchard

MANAGING EDITOR: Vince Janoski

DESIGNER: Daniel Williams

This edition published by Spark Publishing

Spark Publishing
A Division of SparkNotes LLC
120 Fifth Avenue, 8th Floor
New York, NY 10011

03 04 05 06 07 **SN** 9 8 7 6 5 4 3 2 1

Please submit all comments and questions or report errors to *www.sparknotes.com/errors*

Library of Congress Cataloging-in-Publication Data available upon request

Printed and bound in the United States

ISBN 1-58663-847-5 (paperback)
ISBN 1-41140-045-3 (hardcover)

There's matter in these sighs, these profound heaves.
You must translate: 'tis fit we understand them.

(*Hamlet*, 4.1.1–2)

FEAR NOT.

Have you ever found yourself looking at a Shakespeare play, then down at the footnotes, then back at the play, and still not understanding? You know what the individual words mean, but they don't add up. SparkNotes' *No Fear Shakespeare* will help you break through all that. Put the pieces together with our easy-to-read translations. Soon you'll be reading Shakespeare's own words fearlessly—and actually enjoying it.

No Fear Shakespeare puts Shakespeare's language side-by-side with a facing-page translation into modern English— the kind of English people actually speak today. When Shakespeare's words make your head spin, our translation will help you sort out what's happening, who's saying what, and why.

JULIUS CAESAR

CHARACTERS

Julius Caesar—A great Roman general who has recently returned to Rome after a military victory in Spain. Julius Caesar is not the main character of the play that bears his name; Brutus has over four times as many lines, and the play does not show us Caesar's point of view. Nonetheless, virtually every other character is preoccupied with Caesar—specifically, with the possibility that Caesar may soon become king. If Caesar were to become king, it would mean the end of Rome's republican system of government, in which senators, representing the citizens of Rome, wield most of the power. To noblemen like Brutus and Cassius, who consider themselves the equals of Caesar or any other citizen, Caesar's coronation would mean they would no longer be free men but rather slaves. Caesar never explicitly says that he wants to be king—he even refuses the crown three times in a dramatic public display—but everything he says and does demonstrates that he regards himself as special and superior to other mortals. In his own mind, he seems already to be an absolute ruler.

Brutus—A high-ranking, well-regarded Roman nobleman who participates in a conspiracy to assassinate Caesar. Brutus is motivated by his sense of honor, which requires him to place the good of Rome above his own personal interests or feelings. Thus, he plots against Caesar in order to preserve the republic even though he loves and admires Caesar personally. While the other conspirators act out of envy and rivalry, only Brutus truly believes that Caesar's death will benefit Rome. Brutus's sense of honor is also his weakness, as he tends to assume that his fellow Romans are as highminded as he is, which makes it easy for others to manipulate him.

Antony—A loyal friend of Caesar's. In contrast to the self-disciplined Brutus, Antony is notoriously impulsive and pleasure-seeking, passionate rather than principled. He is extremely spontaneous and lives in the present moment. As resourceful as he is unscrupulous, Antony proves to be a dangerous enemy of Brutus and the other conspirators.

Cassius—A talented general and longtime acquaintance of Caesar. Cassius resents the fact that the Roman populace has come to revere Caesar almost as a god. He slyly leads Brutus to believe that Caesar has become too powerful and must die, finally converting Brutus to his cause by sending him forged letters claiming that the Roman people support the death of Caesar. Impulsive and unscrupulous like Antony, Cassius harbors no illusions about the way the political world works. A shrewd opportunist, he acts effectively but lacks integrity.

Octavius—Caesar's adopted son and appointed successor. Octavius, who had been traveling abroad, returns after Caesar's death, then joins with Antony and sets off to fight Cassius and Brutus. Antony tries to control Octavius's movements, but Octavius follows his adopted father's example and emerges as the authoritative figure, paving the way for his eventual seizure of the reins of Roman government.

Casca—One of the conspirators. Casca is a tribune (an official elected to represent the common people of Rome) who resents Caesar's ambition. A rough and blunt-speaking man, Casca relates to Cassius and Brutus how Antony offered the crown to Caesar three times and how each time Caesar declined it. Casca insists, however, that Caesar was acting, manipulating the populace into believing that he has no personal ambition. Casca is the first to stab Caesar.

Calphurnia—Caesar's wife. Calphurnia invests great authority in omens and portents. She warns Caesar against going to the Senate on the Ides of March, for she has had terrible nightmares and heard reports of many bad omens.

Portia—Brutus's wife and the daughter of a noble Roman (Cato) who took sides against Caesar. Portia, accustomed to being Brutus's confidante, is upset to find him so reluctant to speak his mind when she finds him troubled.

Flavius and **Murellus**—Two tribunes who condemn the plebeians for their fickleness in cheering Caesar when once they cheered for Caesar's enemy Pompey. Flavius and Murellus are punished for removing the decorations from Caesar's statues during Caesar's triumphal parade.

Cicero—A Roman senator renowned for his oratorical skill. Cicero speaks at Caesar's triumphal parade. He later dies at the order of Antony, Octavius, and Lepidus.

Lepidus—The third member of Antony and Octavius's coalition. Though Antony has a low opinion of Lepidus, Octavius trusts Lepidus's loyalty.

Decius—A member of the conspiracy. Decius convinces Caesar that Calphurnia misinterpreted her dire nightmares and that, in fact, no danger awaits him at the Senate. Decius leads Caesar right into the hands of the conspirators.

NO FEAR SHAKESPEARE

JULIUS CAESAR

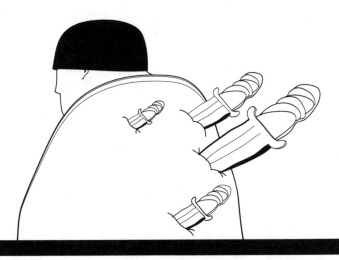

ACT ONE
SCENE 1

Enter FLAVIUS, MURELLUS, *a* CARPENTER, *a* COBBLER, *and certain other* COMMONERS *over the stage*

FLAVIUS
    Hence! Home, you idle creatures get you home!
    Is this a holiday? What, know you not,
    Being mechanical, you ought not walk
    Upon a laboring day without the sign
5   Of your profession?—Speak, what trade art thou?

CARPENTER
    Why, sir, a carpenter.

MURELLUS
    Where is thy leather apron and thy rule?
    What dost thou with thy best apparel on?
    —You, sir, what trade are you?

COBBLER
10   Truly, sir, in respect of a fine workman, I am but, as you
    would say, a cobbler.

MURELLUS
    But what trade art thou? Answer me directly.

COBBLER
    A trade, sir, that I hope I may use with a safe conscience,
    which is, indeed, sir, a mender of bad soles.

MURELLUS
15   What trade, thou knave? Thou naughty knave, what trade?

COBBLER
    Nay, I beseech you, sir, be not out with me. Yet, if you be
    out, sir, I can mend you.

MURELLUS
    What mean'st thou by that? "Mend" me, thou saucy
    fellow?

ACT ONE
SCENE 1

FLAVIUS *and* MURELLUS *enter and speak to a*
CARPENTER, *a* COBBLER, *and some other commoners.*

FLAVIUS

Get out of here! Go home, you lazy men. What, is
today a holiday? Don't you know that working men
aren't supposed to walk around on a workday without
wearing their work clothes? You there, speak up.
What's your occupation?

CARPENTER

I'm a carpenter, sir.

MURELLUS

Where are your leather apron and your ruler? What
are you doing, wearing your best clothes? And you,
sir, what's *your* trade?

COBBLER

Well, compared to a fine workman, you might call me
a mere cobbler.

MURELLUS

But what's your trade? Answer me straightforwardly.

COBBLER

It is a trade, sir, that I practice with a clear conscience.
I am a mender of worn soles.

MURELLUS

What trade, boy? You insolent rascal, what trade?

COBBLER

Sir, please, don't be angry. But if your soles are worn
out, I can mend you.

MURELLUS

What do you mean by that? "Mend" me, you imper-
tinent fellow?!

COBBLER
20   Why, sir, cobble you.

FLAVIUS
        Thou art a cobbler, art thou?

COBBLER
        Truly, sir, all that I live by is with the awl. I meddle with no
        tradesman's matters nor women's matters, but withal I am
        indeed, sir, a surgeon to old shoes. When they are in great
25   danger, I recover them. As proper men as ever trod upon
        neat's leather have gone upon my handiwork.

FLAVIUS
        But wherefore art not in thy shop today?
        Why dost thou lead these men about the streets?

COBBLER
        Truly, sir, to wear out their shoes to get myself into more
30   work. But indeed, sir, we make holiday to see Caesar and to
        rejoice in his triumph.

MURELLUS
        Wherefore rejoice? What conquest brings he home?
        What tributaries follow him to Rome
        To grace in captive bonds his chariot wheels?
35   You blocks, you stones, you worse than senseless things,
        O you hard hearts, you cruèl men of Rome,
        Knew you not Pompey? Many a time and oft
        Have you climbed up to walls and battlements,
        To towers and windows, yea, to chimney tops,
40   Your infants in your arms, and there have sat
        The livelong day with patient expectation
        To see great Pompey pass the streets of Rome.
        And when you saw his chariot but appear,
        Have you not made an universal shout
45   That Tiber trembled underneath her banks
        To hear the replication of your sounds
        Made in her concave shores?
        And do you now put on your best attire?
        And do you now cull out a holiday?

COBBLER

Cobble you, sir.

FLAVIUS

You're a cobbler, are you?

COBBLER

Sir, I make my living using an awl. I stick to my work; I don't meddle in politics or chase women. I'm a surgeon to old shoes. When they're endangered, I save them. The noblest men who ever walked on leather have walked on my handiwork.

FLAVIUS

But why aren't you in your shop today? Why are you leading these men through the streets?

COBBLER

Well, to wear out their shoes and get myself more work. Seriously, though, we took the day off to see Caesar, sir, and celebrate his triumph.

MURELLUS

Why would you celebrate it? What victory does he bring home? What foreign lands has he conquered and captive foreigners chained to his chariot wheels? You blockheads, you unfeeling men! You hard hearts, you cruel men of Rome, didn't you know Pompey? Many times you climbed up on walls and battlements, towers and windows—even chimney tops—with your babies in your arms, and sat there patiently all day waiting to see great Pompey ride through the streets of Rome. And when you caught a glimpse of his chariot, didn't you shout so loud that the river Tiber shook as it echoed? And now you put on your best clothes? And now you take a holiday?

Caesar has just conquered the sons of his deceased enemy Pompey. He as won in a civil war, not a foreign conquest.

50   And do you now strew flowers in his way
        That comes in triumph over Pompey's blood?
        Be gone!
        Run to your houses, fall upon your knees,
        Pray to the gods to intermit the plague
55   That needs must light on this ingratitude.

FLAVIUS
        Go, go, good countrymen, and for this fault,
        Assemble all the poor men of your sort,
        Draw them to Tiber banks, and weep your tears
        Into the channel till the lowest stream
60   Do kiss the most exalted shores of all.

Exeunt CARPENTER, COBBLER, *and all the other commoners*

        See whether their basest metal be not moved.
        They vanish tongue-tied in their guiltiness.
        Go you down that way towards the Capitol.
        This way will I. Disrobe the images
65   If you do find them decked with ceremonies.

MURELLUS
        May we do so?
        You know it is the feast of Lupercal.

FLAVIUS
        It is no matter. Let no images
        Be hung with Caesar's trophies. I'll about
70   And drive away the vulgar from the streets.
        So do you too, where you perceive them thick.
        These growing feathers plucked from Caesar's wing
        Will make him fly an ordinary pitch,
        Who else would soar above the view of men
75   And keep us all in servile fearfulness.

Exeunt severally

And now you toss flowers in the path of Caesar, who comes in triumph over Pompey's defeated sons? Go home! Run to your houses, fall on your knees, and pray to the gods to spare you the pain that you deserve for such ingratitude.

FLAVIUS

Go, go, good countrymen, and to make up for having done wrong, gather up all the poor men like your-selves, lead them to the Tiber, and weep into the river until it overflows its banks.

The CARPENTER, COBBLER, *and all the commoners exit.*

Well, that ought to move even the most thickheaded of them. There they go, feeling so guilty they're now tongue-tied—they don't have a thing to say. You go down toward the Capitol, and I'll go this way. Undress the statues if they're decorated in honor of Caesar.

MURELLUS

The feast of Luper-cal is an annual celebration to honor the Roman god Lupercus (called Pan in Greek mythology).

Can we do that? You know it's the feast of Lupercal.

FLAVIUS

It doesn't matter. Make sure that none of the statues are decorated in tribute to Caesar. I'll walk around and force the commoners off the streets. You do the same, wherever the crowds are thick. If we take away Caesar's support, he'll have to come back down to earth; otherwise, he'll fly too high and keep the rest of us in a state of fear and obedience.

They exit in different directions.

ACT 1, SCENE 2

Flourish
Enter CAESAR, ANTONY, *dressed for the course,* CALPHURNIA,
PORTIA, DECIUS, CICERO, BRUTUS, CASSIUS, CASCA, *and a*
SOOTHSAYER *in a throng of plebians.*
After them, MURELLUS *and* FLAVIUS

CAESAR
Calphurnia!

CASCA
Peace, ho! Caesar speaks.

CAESAR
Calphurnia!

CALPHURNIA
Here, my lord.

CAESAR
5   Stand you directly in Antonius' way
When he doth run his course.—Antonius!

ANTONY
Caesar, my lord.

CAESAR
Forget not in your speed, Antonius,
To touch Calphurnia, for our elders say
10   The barren, touchèd in this holy chase,
Shake off their sterile curse.

ANTONY
                 I shall remember.
When Caesar says, "do this," it is performed.

CAESAR
Set on, and leave no ceremony out.

Music

SOOTHSAYER
Caesar!

ACT 1, SCENE 2

A trumpet sounds. CAESAR *enters, followed by* ANTONY,
dressed formally for a foot race, then CALPHURNIA,
PORTIA, DECIUS, CICERO, BRUTUS, CASSIUS, *and* CASCA.
A great crowd follows, among them a SOOTHSAYER.

A soothsayer is a fortune-teller.

CAESAR

Calphurnia!

CASCA

Quiet! Caesar's talking.

CAESAR

Calphurnia!

CALPHURNIA

I'm here, my lord.

CAESAR

Stand right in Antonius's path when he runs the race.
Antonius!

ANTONY

Yes, Caesar?

CAESAR

Antonius, after you take off, don't forget to touch Calphurnia, because our wise elders say that if you touch
an infertile woman during this holy race, she'll be
freed from the curse of sterility.

ANTONY

I'll remember. When Caesar says "do this," it is done.

CAESAR

Continue, then, and don't forget to perform all of the
rituals.

A trumpet plays.

SOOTHSAYER

Caesar!

CAESAR

15   Ha! Who calls?

CASCA

Bid every noise be still. Peace yet again.

Music ceases

CAESAR

Who is it in the press that calls on me?
I hear a tongue, shriller than all the music,
Cry "Caesar!"—Speak. Caesar is turned to hear.

SOOTHSAYER

20   Beware the ides of March.

CAESAR

What man is that?

BRUTUS

A soothsayer bids you beware the ides of March.

CAESAR

Set him before me. Let me see his face.

CASSIUS

Fellow, come from the throng. Look upon Caesar.

SOOTHSAYER *approaches*

CAESAR

What sayst thou to me now? Speak once again.

SOOTHSAYER

25   Beware the ides of March.

CAESAR

He is a dreamer. Let us leave him. Pass!

Sennet. Exeunt. Manent **BRUTUS** *and* **CASSIUS**

CASSIUS

Will you go see the order of the course?

CAESAR

Who's calling me?

CASCA

Quiet, everyone! Quiet!

The trumpet stops playing.

CAESAR

Who in the crowd is calling me? I hear a voice more piercing than the music of these trumpets calling "Caesar!" Speak. Caesar is listening.

SOOTHSAYER

Beware of March 15th.

CAESAR

Who's that?

BRUTUS

A soothsayer tells you to beware of March 15th.

CAESAR

Bring him in front of me. Let me see his face.

CASSIUS

You, fellow, step out of the crowd. This is Caesar you're looking at.

The **soothsayer** *approaches.*

CAESAR

What do you have to say to me now? Speak once again.

SOOTHSAYER

Beware of March 15th.

CAESAR

He's insane. Let's leave him. Let's move.

Trumpets play. Everyone exits except
brutus *and* **cassius.**

CASSIUS

Are you going to watch the race?

BRUTUS
Not I.

CASSIUS
I pray you, do.

BRUTUS
30   I am not gamesome. I do lack some part
Of that quick spirit that is in Antony.
Let me not hinder, Cassius, your desires.
I'll leave you.

CASSIUS
Brutus, I do observe you now of late
35   I have not from your eyes that gentleness
And show of love as I was wont to have.
You bear too stubborn and too strange a hand
Over your friend that loves you.

BRUTUS
                         Cassius,
Be not deceived. If I have veiled my look,
40   I turn the trouble of my countenance
Merely upon myself. Vexèd I am
Of late with passions of some difference,
Conceptions only proper to myself,
Which give some soil perhaps to my behaviors.
45   But let not therefore, my good friends, be grieved—
Among which number, Cassius, be you one—
Nor construe any further my neglect
Than that poor Brutus, with himself at war,
Forgets the shows of love to other men.

CASSIUS
50   Then, Brutus, I have much mistook your passion,
By means whereof this breast of mine hath buried
Thoughts of great value, worthy cogitations.
Tell me, good Brutus, can you see your face?

BRUTUS
No, Cassius, for the eye sees not itself
55   But by reflection, by some other things.

BRUTUS

Not me.

CASSIUS

Please, come.

BRUTUS

I don't like sports. I'm not competitive like Antony. But don't let me keep you from going, Cassius. I'll go my own way.

CASSIUS

Brutus, I've been watching you lately. You seem less good-natured and affectionate toward me than usual. You've been stubborn and unfamiliar with me, your friend who loves you.

BRUTUS

Cassius, don't take it badly. If I seem guarded, it's only because I'm uneasy with *myself*. Lately I've been overwhelmed with private thoughts and inner conflicts, which have affected my behavior. But this shouldn't trouble my good friends—and I consider you a good friend, Cassius. Don't think anything more about my distraction than that poor Brutus, who is at war with himself, forgets to show affection to others.

CASSIUS

Brutus, I misunderstood your feelings, and therefore kept to myself certain thoughts I might have shared. Tell me, good Brutus, can you see your face?

BRUTUS

No, Cassius. The eye can't see itself, except by reflection in other surfaces.

CASSIUS

'Tis just.
And it is very much lamented, Brutus,
That you have no such mirrors as will turn
Your hidden worthiness into your eye
60 That you might see your shadow. I have heard
Where many of the best respect in Rome,
Except immortal Caesar, speaking of Brutus
And groaning underneath this age's yoke,
Have wished that noble Brutus had his eyes.

BRUTUS

65 Into what dangers would you lead me, Cassius,
That you would have me seek into myself
For that which is not in me?

CASSIUS

Therefore, good Brutus, be prepared to hear.
And since you know you cannot see yourself
70 So well as by reflection, I, your glass,
Will modestly discover to yourself
That of yourself which you yet know not of.
And be not jealous on me, gentle Brutus.
Were I a common laugher, or did use
75 To stale with ordinary oaths my love
To every new protester, if you know
That I do fawn on men and hug them hard
And, after, scandal them, or if you know
That I profess myself in banqueting
80 To all the rout, then hold me dangerous.

Flourish, and shout within

BRUTUS

What means this shouting? I do fear, the people
Choose Caesar for their king.

CASSIUS

Ay, do you fear it?
Then must I think you would not have it so.

CASSIUS

That's true. And it's too bad, Brutus, that you don't have any mirrors that could display your hidden excellence to yourself. I've heard many of the noblest Romans—next to immortal Caesar—speaking of you, complaining of the tyranny of today's government, and wishing that your eyes were working better.

BRUTUS

What dangers are you trying to lead me into, Cassius, that you want me to look inside myself for something that's not there?

CASSIUS

I'll tell you, good Brutus. And since you know you can see yourself best by reflection, I'll be your mirror and show you, without exaggeration, things inside you that you can't see. And don't be suspicious of me, noble Brutus. If I were your average fool, or if I made my feelings for you worthless by making the same promises of friendship to everybody, or if you'd seen me first flattering men, hugging them tightly, and later slandering them behind their backs, or if you hear that I drunkenly declare friendship at banquets with all the rabble, only then, of course, go ahead and assume I'm dangerous.

Trumpets play offstage, and then a shout is heard.

BRUTUS

Why are they shouting? I'm afraid the people have made Caesar their king.

CASSIUS

Really, are you afraid of that? Then I have to assume you don't want him to be king.

BRUTUS

I would not, Cassius. Yet I love him well.
85 But wherefore do you hold me here so long?
What is it that you would impart to me?
If it be aught toward the general good,
Set honor in one eye and death i' th' other,
And I will look on both indifferently,
90 For let the gods so speed me as I love
The name of honor more than I fear death.

CASSIUS

I know that virtue to be in you, Brutus,
As well as I do know your outward favor.
Well, honor is the subject of my story.
95 I cannot tell what you and other men
Think of this life, but, for my single self,
I had as lief not be as live to be
In awe of such a thing as I myself.
I was born free as Caesar. So were you.
100 We both have fed as well, and we can both
Endure the winter's cold as well as he.
For once upon a raw and gusty day,
The troubled Tiber chafing with her shores,
Caesar said to me, "Darest thou, Cassius, now
105 Leap in with me into this angry flood
And swim to yonder point?" Upon the word,
Accoutred as I was, I plungèd in
And bade him follow. So indeed he did.
The torrent roared, and we did buffet it
110 With lusty sinews, throwing it aside
And stemming it with hearts of controversy.
But ere we could arrive the point proposed,
Caesar cried, "Help me, Cassius, or I sink!"
I, as Aeneas, our great ancestor,
115 Did from the flames of Troy upon his shoulder
The old Anchises bear, so from the waves of Tiber
Did I the tired Caesar. And this man

BRUTUS

I don't, Cassius, though I love Caesar very much. But why do you keep me here so long? What do you want to tell me? If it's for the good of all Romans, I'd do it even if it meant my death. Let the gods give me good luck only as long as I love honor more than I fear death.

CASSIUS

I know this quality in you, Brutus—it's as familiar to me as your face. Indeed, honor is what I want to talk to you about. I don't know what you and other men think of this life, but as for me, I'd rather not live at all than live to worship a man as ordinary as myself. I was born as free as Caesar. So were you. We both have eaten as well, and we can both endure the cold winter as well as he. Once, on a cold and windy day, when the river Tiber was crashing against its banks, Caesar said to me, "Cassius, I dare you to jump into this rough water with me and swim to that point there." As soon as he spoke, though I was fully dressed, I plunged in and called for him to follow. And he did. The water roared, and we fought against it with vigorous arms. And, thanks to our fierce competitiveness, we made progress. But before we reached the end point, Caesar cried, "Help me, Cassius, or I will sink!" And just as Aeneas, the hero who founded Rome, emerged from the fires of Troy with his elderly father Anchises on his shoulder, so I emerged from the Tiber carrying the tired Caesar.

Is now become a god, and Cassius is
A wretched creature and must bend his body
120   If Caesar carelessly but nod on him.
He had a fever when he was in Spain,
And when the fit was on him, I did mark
How he did shake. 'Tis true, this god did shake!
His coward lips did from their color fly,
125   And that same eye whose bend doth awe the world
Did lose his luster. I did hear him groan,
Ay, and that tongue of his that bade the Romans
Mark him and write his speeches in their books—
"Alas," it cried, "give me some drink, Titinius,"
130   As a sick girl. Ye gods, it doth amaze me
A man of such a feeble temper should
So get the start of the majestic world
And bear the palm alone.

Shout within. Flourish

BRUTUS
                                    Another general shout!
I do believe that these applauses are
135   For some new honors that are heaped on Caesar.

CASSIUS
Why, man, he doth bestride the narrow world
Like a Colossus, and we petty men
Walk under his huge legs and peep about
To find ourselves dishonorable graves.
140   Men at some time are masters of their fates.
The fault, dear Brutus, is not in our stars
But in ourselves, that we are underlings.
Brutus and Caesar—what should be in that "Caesar"?
Why should that name be sounded more than yours?
145   Write them together, yours is as fair a name.
Sound them, it doth become the mouth as well.
Weigh them, it is as heavy. Conjure with 'em,

And this is the man who has now become a god, and I'm a wretched creature who must bow down if Caesar so much as carelessly nods my way. In Spain, Caesar had a fever, and it made him shake. It's true, this so-called "god"—he shook. His cowardly lips turned white, and the same eye whose gaze terrifies the world lost its gleam. I heard him groan—yes, I did—and the same tongue that ordered the Romans to obey him and transcribe his speeches in their books cried, "Give me some water, Titinius," like a sick girl. It astounds me that such a weak man could beat the whole world and carry the trophy of victory alone.

A shout offstage. Trumpets play.

BRUTUS

More shouting! I think this applause is for some new honors awarded to Caesar.

CASSIUS

Why, Caesar straddles the narrow world like a giant, and we petty men walk under his huge legs and look forward only to dying dishonorably, as slaves. Men can be masters of their fate. It is not destiny's fault, but our own faults, that we're slaves. "Brutus" and "Caesar." What's so special about "Caesar"? Why should that name be proclaimed more than yours? Write them together—yours is just as good a name. Pronounce them—it is just as nice to say. Weigh them—it's just as heavy.

"Brutus" will start a spirit as soon as "Caesar."
Now in the names of all the gods at once,
150 Upon what meat doth this our Caesar feed
That he is grown so great? Age, thou art shamed!
Rome, thou hast lost the breed of noble bloods!
When went there by an age, since the great flood,
But it was famed with more than with one man?
155 When could they say till now, that talked of Rome,
That her wide walks encompassed but one man?
Now is it Rome indeed, and room enough,
When there is in it but one only man.
Oh, you and I have heard our fathers say,
160 There was a Brutus once that would have brooked
Th' eternal devil to keep his state in Rome
As easily as a king.

BRUTUS
That you do love me, I am nothing jealous.
What you would work me to, I have some aim.
165 How I have thought of this and of these times
I shall recount hereafter. For this present,
I would not, so with love I might entreat you,
Be any further moved. What you have said
I will consider, what you have to say
170 I will with patience hear, and find a time
Both meet to hear and answer such high things.
Till then, my noble friend, chew upon this:
Brutus had rather be a villager
Than to repute himself a son of Rome
175 Under these hard conditions as this time
Is like to lay upon us.

CASSIUS
                            I am glad that my weak words
Have struck but thus much show of fire from Brutus.

Enter CAESAR *and his train, which includes* CASCA

Cast spells with them, and "Brutus" will call up a ghost as well as "Caesar." Now, in the name of all the gods, I ask you what food does Caesar eat that has made him grow so great? Our era should be ashamed! Rome has lost the ability to raise noble men! When was there ever an age, since the beginning of time, that didn't feature more than one famous man? Until now, no one could say that only one man mattered in all of vast Rome. Now, though, in all of Rome, there's room for only one man. You and I have heard our fathers talk of another Brutus—your ancestor—who would've let the devil himself reign in his Roman Republic before he let a king rule.

BRUTUS

I have no doubt that you love me. I'm beginning to understand what you want me to do. What I think about this, and about what's happening here in Rome, I'll tell you later. For now, don't try to persuade me anymore—I ask you as a friend. I'll think over what you've said, I'll listen patiently to whatever else you have to say, and I'll find a good time for us to discuss further such weighty matters. Until then, my noble friend, think about this: I'd rather be a poor villager than call myself a citizen of Rome under the hard conditions that this time is likely to put us through.

CASSIUS

I'm glad that my weak words have provoked even this small show of protest from you.

CAESAR *enters with his followers, who include* CASCA.

BRUTUS
> The games are done and Caesar is returning.

CASSIUS
> As they pass by, pluck Casca by the sleeve,
180 > And he will, after his sour fashion, tell you
> What hath proceeded worthy note today.

BRUTUS
> I will do so. But, look you, Cassius,
> The angry spot doth glow on Caesar's brow,
> And all the rest look like a chidden train.
185 > Calphurnia's cheek is pale, and Cicero
> Looks with such ferret and such fiery eyes
> As we have seen him in the Capitol
> Being crossed in conference by some senators.

CASSIUS
> Casca will tell us what the matter is.

> *During the exchange between* CAESAR *and* ANTONY, BRUTUS
> *pulls* CASCA *by the sleeve*

CAESAR
190 > Antonio.

ANTONY
> Caesar.

CAESAR
> *(aside to* ANTONY*)* Let me have men about me that are fat,
> Sleek-headed men and such as sleep a-nights.
> Yond Cassius has a lean and hungry look.
195 > He thinks too much. Such men are dangerous.

ANTONY
> *(aside to* CAESAR*)* Fear him not, Caesar. He's not dangerous.
> He is a noble Roman and well given.

BRUTUS

The games are done and Caesar is returning.

CASSIUS

As they pass by, grab Casca by the sleeve, and he'll tell you if anything important happened today—in his usual sour way.

BRUTUS

I'll do so. But look, Cassius, Caesar looks angry and everyone else looks as if they've been scolded. Calphurnia's face is pale, and Cicero's eyes are as red and fiery as they get when senators are arguing with him at the Capitol.

CASSIUS

Casca will tell us what's the matter.

During the exchange between CAESAR *and* ANTONY, BRUTUS *pulls* CASCA *by the sleeve.*

CAESAR

Antonio!

ANTONY

Caesar?

CAESAR

(speaking so that only ANTONY *can hear)* I want the men around me to be fat, healthy-looking men who sleep at night. That Cassius over there has a lean and hungry look. He thinks too much. Men like him are dangerous.

ANTONY

(speaking so that only CAESAR *can hear)* Don't be afraid of him, Caesar. He isn't dangerous. He's a noble Roman with a good disposition.

CAESAR
(*aside to* **ANTONY**) Would he were fatter! But I fear him not.
Yet if my name were liable to fear,
200   I do not know the man I should avoid
So soon as that spare Cassius. He reads much.
He is a great observer, and he looks
Quite through the deeds of men. He loves no plays,
As thou dost, Antony. He hears no music.
205   Seldom he smiles, and smiles in such a sort
As if he mocked himself and scorned his spirit
That could be moved to smile at anything.
Such men as he be never at heart's ease
Whiles they behold a greater than themselves,
210   And therefore are they very dangerous.
I rather tell thee what is to be feared
Than what I fear, for always I am Caesar.
Come on my right hand, for this ear is deaf,
And tell me truly what thou think'st of him.

Sennet. Exeunt **CAESAR** *and all his train except* **CASCA**

CASCA
(*to* **BRUTUS**)
215   You pulled me by the cloak. Would you speak with me?

BRUTUS
Ay, Casca. Tell us what hath chanced today
That Caesar looks so sad.

CASCA
Why, you were with him, were you not?

BRUTUS
I should not then ask Casca what had chanced.

CASCA
220   Why, there was a crown offered him; and, being offered
him, he put it by with the back of his hand, thus; and then
the people fell a-shouting.

CAESAR

(speaking so that only ANTONY *can hear)* I wish he were fatter! But I'm not afraid of him. And yet, if I were capable of fearing anyone, Cassius would be the first man I'd avoid. He reads a lot, he's a keen observer, and he sees the hidden motives in what men do. He doesn't like plays the way you do, Antony. He doesn't listen to music. He rarely smiles, and when he does smile, he does so in a self-mocking way, as if he scorns himself for smiling at all. Men like him will never be comfortable while someone ranks higher than themselves, and therefore they're very dangerous. I'm telling you what should be feared, not what I fear—because after all, I am Caesar. Come over to my right side, because this ear is deaf, and tell me what you really think of Cassius.

Trumpets play.
> CAESAR *exits with all his followers except* CASCA.

CASCA

(to BRUTUS*)* You tugged on my cloak. Do you want to speak with me?

BRUTUS

Yes, Casca. Tell us what happened today that put Caesar in such a serious mood.

CASCA

But you were with him, weren't you?

BRUTUS

If I were, I wouldn't need to ask you what happened.

CASCA

A crown was offered to him, and he pushed it away with the back of his hand, like this—and then the people started shouting.

BRUTUS
What was the second noise for?

CASCA
Why, for that too.

CASSIUS
225   They shouted thrice. What was the last cry for?

CASCA
Why, for that too.

BRUTUS
Was the crown offered him thrice?

CASCA
Ay, marry, was 't, and he put it by thrice, every time gentler
than other, and at every putting-by mine honest neighbors
230   shouted.

CASSIUS
Who offered him the crown?

CASCA
                                    Why, Antony.

BRUTUS
Tell us the manner of it, gentle Casca.

CASCA
I can as well be hanged as tell the manner of it. It was mere
foolery. I did not mark it. I saw Mark Antony offer him a
235   crown (yet 'twas not a crown neither, 'twas one of these
coronets) and, as I told you, he put it by once—but, for all
that, to my thinking, he would fain have had it. Then he
offered it to him again, then he put it by again—but, to my
thinking, he was very loath to lay his fingers off it. And then
240   he offered it the third time. He put it the third time by. And
still, as he refused it, the rabblement hooted and clapped
their chapped hands and threw up their sweaty night-caps
and uttered such a deal of stinking breath because Caesar
refused the crown that it had almost choked Caesar—for he
245   swooned and fell down at it. And for mine own part, I durst
not laugh for fear of opening my lips and receiving the bad
air.

BRUTUS

What was the second noise for?

CASCA

The same thing.

CASSIUS

They shouted three times. What was the last cry for?

CASCA

For the same thing.

BRUTUS

The crown was offered to him three times?

CASCA

Yes, indeed, it was, and he pushed it away three times, each time more gently than the last; and at each refusal my countrymen shouted.

CASSIUS

Who offered him the crown?

CASCA

Antony.

BRUTUS

Tell us how it happened, noble Casca.

CASCA

I can't explain it. It was all silly and so I paid no attention. I saw Mark Antony offer him a crown—though it wasn't a real crown, just a small circlet—and, as I told you, he refused it once—though in my opinion he would've liked to have it. Then Antony offered it to him again, and he refused it again (though, in my opinion, he was reluctant to take his hand off it). Then Antony offered it the third time. He refused it the third time, and as he refused it the commoners hooted and clapped their chapped hands, and threw up their sweaty hats, and let loose such a great deal of stinking breath because Caesar refused the crown that it nearly choked Caesar, because he fainted and fell down. As for myself, I didn't dare laugh, for fear of opening my lips and inhaling the stinking air.

CASSIUS
But soft, I pray you. What, did Caesar swoon?

CASCA
He fell down in the marketplace, and foamed at mouth, and
250   was speechless.

BRUTUS
'Tis very like. He hath the falling sickness.

CASSIUS
No, Caesar hath it not. But you and I
And honest Casca, we have the falling sickness.

CASCA
I know not what you mean by that, but I am sure Caesar fell
255   down. If the tag-rag people did not clap him and hiss him
according as he pleased and displeased them, as they use to
do the players in the theatre, I am no true man.

BRUTUS
What said he when he came unto himself?

CASCA
Marry, before he fell down, when he perceived the common
260   herd was glad he refused the crown, he plucked me ope his
doublet and offered them his throat to cut. An I had been a
man of any occupation, if I would not have taken him at a
word, I would I might go to hell among the rogues. And so
he fell. When he came to himself again, he said, if he had
265   done or said anything amiss, he desired their worships to
think it was his infirmity. Three or four wenches where I
stood cried, "Alas, good soul!" and forgave him with all
their hearts. But there's no heed to be taken of them. If
Caesar had stabbed their mothers they would have done no
270   less.

BRUTUS
And after that he came thus sad away?

CASCA
Ay.

CASSIUS

But wait a minute, please. Did you say Caesar fainted?

CASCA

He fell down in the marketplace and foamed at the mouth and was speechless.

BRUTUS

That's very likely. He has epilepsy, a disease where you fall down.

CASSIUS

No, Caesar doesn't have epilepsy. You and I, and honest Casca, we have epilepsy—we've fallen.

CASCA

I don't know what you mean by that, but I'm sure Caesar fell down. The rabble applauded and hissed him according to whether he pleased them or displeased them, just like they do to actors in the theater. If they didn't, I'm a liar.

BRUTUS

What did he say when he regained consciousness?

CASCA

Indeed, before he fell down, when he realized the commoners were glad he refused the crown, he pulled open his robe and offered them his throat to cut. If I'd been a common laborer and hadn't taken him up on his offer, to hell with me. And so he fainted. When he regained consciousness again, he said that if he'd done or said anything wrong, he wanted them to know that it was all because of his sickness. Three or four women near me cried, "Alas, good soul!" and forgave him with all their hearts. But never mind them—if Caesar had stabbed their mothers, they would've forgiven him.

BRUTUS

And after that he came back here looking so serious?

CASCA

Yes.

CASSIUS
Did Cicero say anything?

CASCA
Ay, he spoke Greek.

CASSIUS
275 To what effect?

CASCA
Nay, an I tell you that, I'll ne'er look you i' th' face again.
But those that understood him smiled at one another and
shook their heads. But, for mine own part, it was Greek to
me. I could tell you more news too. Murellus and Flavius,
280 for pulling scarfs off Caesar's images, are put to silence.
Fare you well. There was more foolery yet, if I could
remember it.

CASSIUS
Will you sup with me tonight, Casca?

CASCA
No, I am promised forth.

CASSIUS
285 Will you dine with me tomorrow?

CASCA
Ay, if I be alive and your mind hold and your dinner worth
the eating.

CASSIUS
Good. I will expect you.

CASCA
Do so. Farewell both.

Exit CASCA

BRUTUS
290 What a blunt fellow is this grown to be!
He was quick mettle when he went to school.

CASSIUS

Did Cicero say anything?

CASCA

Yes, he said something in Greek.

CASSIUS

What did he say?

CASCA

If I told you I understood Greek, I'd be lying. But those who understood him smiled at one another and shook their heads. As for myself, it was Greek to me. I have more news too. Murellus and Flavius have been punished for pulling scarves off statues of Caesar. There you go. There was even more foolishness, if I could only remember it.

CASSIUS

Will you have dinner with me tonight, Casca?

CASCA

No, I have a commitment.

CASSIUS

Will you dine with me tomorrow?

CASCA

Yes, if I'm still alive, and you're still sane, and your dinner is worth eating.

CASSIUS

Good. I'll expect you.

CASCA

Do so. Farewell to you both.

CASCA *exits.*

BRUTUS

What a stupid man he's become! He was so sharp when he was in school.

CASSIUS
So is he now in execution
Of any bold or noble enterprise,
However he puts on this tardy form.
295   This rudeness is a sauce to his good wit,
Which gives men stomach to digest his words
With better appetite.

BRUTUS
And so it is. For this time I will leave you.
Tomorrow, if you please to speak with me,
300   I will come home to you. Or, if you will,
Come home to me, and I will wait for you.

CASSIUS
I will do so. Till then, think of the world.

Exit BRUTUS

Well, Brutus, thou art noble. Yet I see
Thy honorable mettle may be wrought
305   From that it is disposed. Therefore it is meet
That noble minds keep ever with their likes,
For who so firm that cannot be seduced?
Caesar doth bear me hard, but he loves Brutus.
If I were Brutus now and he were Cassius,
310   He should not humor me. I will this night,
In several hands, in at his windows throw,
As if they came from several citizens,
Writings all tending to the great opinion
That Rome holds of his name, wherein obscurely
315   Caesar's ambition shall be glancèd at.
And after this let Caesar seat him sure,
For we will shake him, or worse days endure.

Exit

CASSIUS

He's still sharp when it comes to carrying out a bold or noble enterprise, though he puts on this show of stupidity. He speaks roughly, but what he says is smart, and his roughness makes other people enjoy listening to him.

BRUTUS

You're right, that's how it is. I'll leave you for now. If you'd like to talk tomorrow, I'll come to your home. Or, if you don't mind, come to my home, and I'll wait for you.

CASSIUS

I'll do so. Until then, think about the well-being of Rome.

BRUTUS exits.

Well, Brutus, you're noble. Yet I see that your honorable character can be bent from its usual shape, which proves that good men should stick only to the company of other good men, because who is so firm that he can't be seduced? Caesar resents me, but he loves Brutus. If I were Brutus now and Brutus were me, I wouldn't have let him influence me. Tonight I'll throw through his window a few letters in different handwriting—as if they came from several citizens—all testifying to the great respect Romans have for Brutus, and all alluding to Caesar's unseemly ambition. And after this, let Caesar brace himself, for we'll either dethrone him or suffer even worse than now.

CASSIUS exits.

ACT 1, SCENE 3

Thunder and lightning. Enter CASCA *and* CICERO

CICERO
Good even, Casca. Brought you Caesar home?
Why are you breathless? And why stare you so?

CASCA
Are not you moved when all the sway of earth
Shakes like a thing unfirm? O Cicero,
5   I have seen tempests when the scolding winds
Have rived the knotty oaks, and I have seen
Th' ambitious ocean swell and rage and foam
To be exalted with the threatening clouds,
But never till tonight, never till now,
10   Did I go through a tempest dropping fire.
Either there is a civil strife in heaven,
Or else the world, too saucy with the gods,
Incenses them to send destruction.

CICERO
Why, saw you anything more wonderful?

CASCA
15   A common slave—you know him well by sight—
Held up his left hand, which did flame and burn
Like twenty torches joined, and yet his hand,
Not sensible of fire, remained unscorched.
Besides—I ha' not since put up my sword—
20   Against the Capitol I met a lion,
Who glared upon me and went surly by,
Without annoying me. And there were drawn
Upon a heap a hundred ghastly women,
Transformèd with their fear, who swore they saw
25   Men all in fire walk up and down the streets.

ACT 1, SCENE 3

Thunder and lightning. CASCA *and* CICERO *enter.*

CICERO

Good evening, Casca. Did you accompany Caesar home? Why are you breathless, and why are you staring like that?

CASCA

Aren't you disturbed when the earth itself is shaking and swaying as if it were a flimsy thing? Cicero, I've seen storms in which the angry winds split old oak trees, and I've seen the ocean swell, rage, and foam, as if it wanted to reach the storm clouds, but never before tonight, never until now, have I experienced a storm that drops fire. Either there are wars in heaven, or else the world, too insolent toward the gods, provokes them to send destruction.

CICERO

What—have you seen something so strange that it is clearly an omen from the gods?

CASCA

A common slave—you'd know him if you saw him— held up his left hand, which flamed and burned like twenty torches together. And yet his hand was immune to the fire and didn't get burned. Also—I've kept my sword unsheathed since I saw this—in front of the Capitol I met a lion who looked at me and strutted by without bothering to attack me. And there were a hundred spooked women huddled together in fear who swore they saw men on fire walk up and down the streets.

And yesterday the bird of night did sit
Even at noon-day upon the marketplace,
Hooting and shrieking. When these prodigies
Do so conjointly meet, let not men say,
30   "These are their reasons. They are natural."
For I believe they are portentous things
Unto the climate that they point upon.

CICERO
Indeed, it is a strange-disposèd time.
But men may construe things after their fashion,
35   Clean from the purpose of the things themselves.
Comes Caesar to the Capitol tomorrow?

CASCA
He doth, for he did bid Antonius
Send word to you he would be there tomorrow.

CICERO
Good night then, Casca. This disturbèd sky
40   Is not to walk in.

CASCA
Farewell, Cicero.

Exit CICERO

Enter CASSIUS

CASSIUS
Who's there?

CASCA
                              A Roman.

CASSIUS
                                                  Casca, by your voice.

CASCA
Your ear is good. Cassius, what night is this!

CASSIUS
A very pleasing night to honest men.

CASCA
45   Who ever knew the heavens menace so?

And yesterday the night owl sat hooting and shrieking in the marketplace at noon. When all these extraordinary things happen at once, we shouldn't say, "These happenings can be explained rationally. They're natural enough." I think these things are omens of things to come in our country.

CICERO
Indeed, it's a strange time. But men tend to interpret things however suits them and totally miss the actual meaning of the things themselves. Is Caesar visiting the Capitol tomorrow?

CASCA
He is, because he told Antonius to tell you he'd be there tomorrow.

CICERO
Good night then, Casca. This bad weather isn't good to walk around in.

CASCA
Farewell, Cicero.

CICERO *exits.*

CASSIUS *enters.*

CASSIUS
Who's there?

CASCA
A Roman.

CASSIUS
It's Casca—I know your voice.

CASCA
Your ear is good. Cassius, what a night this is!

CASSIUS
It's a very pleasing night to honest men.

CASCA
Who ever saw the heavens threaten like this?

CASSIUS

Those that have known the earth so full of faults.
For my part, I have walked about the streets,
Submitting me unto the perilous night,
And, thus unbracèd, Casca, as you see,
50   Have bared my bosom to the thunder-stone.
And when the cross blue lightning seemed to open
The breast of heaven, I did present myself
Even in the aim and very flash of it.

CASCA

But wherefore did you so much tempt the heavens?
55   It is the part of men to fear and tremble
When the most mighty gods by tokens send
Such dreadful heralds to astonish us.

CASSIUS

You are dull, Casca, and those sparks of life
That should be in a Roman you do want,
60   Or else you use not. You look pale, and gaze,
And put on fear, and cast yourself in wonder
To see the strange impatience of the heavens.
But if you would consider the true cause
Why all these fires, why all these gliding ghosts,
65   Why birds and beasts from quality and kind,
Why old men fool and children calculate,
Why all these things change from their ordinance
Their natures and preformèd faculties
To monstrous quality—why, you shall find
70   That heaven hath infused them with these spirits
To make them instruments of fear and warning
Unto some monstrous state.
Now could I, Casca, name to thee a man
Most like this dreadful night,
75   That thunders, lightens, opens graves, and roars
As doth the lion in the Capitol—

CASSIUS

Those who have known how bad things are here on earth. I have walked around the streets, exposing myself to the perilous night, unbuttoned like this, as you see, Casca, baring my chest to the thunderbolt. When the forked blue lightning seemed to break open the sky, I put myself right where I thought it would hit.

CASCA

But why did you tempt the heavens like that? Mankind's role is to fear and tremble when the almighty gods send warning signals.

CASSIUS

You're acting stupid, Casca, and you lack the quick wits that a Roman should have—or else you don't use them. You go pale, you stare, and you act in awe of the strange disturbance in the heavens. But if you thought about the real reason for all these fires, all these gliding ghosts, for why birds and animals abandon their natural behavior, why old men, fools, and children make predictions, why all sorts of things have departed from the usual course of their natures and become monstrosities, then you'd understand that heaven had them act this way so they would serve as frightening warnings of an unnatural state to come. Right this minute, Casca, I could name a man who's just like this dreadful night. A man who thunders, throws lightning, splits open graves, and roars like the lion in the Capitol.

A man no mightier than thyself or me
In personal action, yet prodigious grown,
And fearful as these strange eruptions are.

CASCA

80   'Tis Caesar that you mean. Is it not, Cassius?

CASSIUS

Let it be who it is. For Romans now
Have thews and limbs like to their ancestors,
But—woe the while!—our fathers' minds are dead,
And we are governed with our mothers' spirits.

85   Our yoke and sufferance show us womanish.

CASCA

Indeed, they say the senators tomorrow
Mean to establish Caesar as a king,
And he shall wear his crown by sea and land
In every place save here in Italy.

CASSIUS

90   I know where I will wear this dagger then.
Cassius from bondage will deliver Cassius.
Therein, ye gods, you make the weak most strong.
Therein, ye gods, you tyrants do defeat.
Nor stony tower, nor walls of beaten brass,

95   Nor airless dungeon, nor strong links of iron
Can be retentive to the strength of spirit.
But life, being weary of these worldly bars,
Never lacks power to dismiss itself.
If I know this, know all the world besides,

100   That part of tyranny that I do bear
I can shake off at pleasure.

Thunder still

CASCA

        So can I.
So every bondman in his own hand bears
The power to cancel his captivity.

A man no mightier than you or I in ability, yet grown as huge and frightening as tonight's strange happenings.

CASCA

You're talking about Caesar, right, Cassius?

CASSIUS

Let it be who it is. Romans today still have the powerful bodies of their ancestors, but, unfortunately, we don't have their manly spirits, and instead we take after our mothers. Our tolerance for slavery and oppression shows us to be weak, like women.

CASCA

Indeed, they say that the senators plan to establish Caesar as a king tomorrow, and he'll wear his crown at sea and on land everywhere except here in Italy.

CASSIUS

I know where I'll wear this dagger, then. I'll kill myself to save myself from slavery. In suicide, gods make the weak strong. In suicide, gods allow tyrants to be defeated. No stony tower, no brass walls, no airless dungeon, no iron chains can contain a strong mind. But if a man becomes weary of these obstacles, he can always kill himself. Let everyone beware: I can shake off the tyranny that now oppresses me whenever I choose.

Thunder continues.

CASCA

So can I. In fact, every imprisoned man holds in his own hand the tool to free himself.

CASSIUS

> And why should Caesar be a tyrant then?
> 105 Poor man! I know he would not be a wolf
> But that he sees the Romans are but sheep.
> He were no lion were not Romans hinds.
> Those that with haste will make a mighty fire
> Begin it with weak straws. What trash is Rome,
> 110 What rubbish and what offal, when it serves
> For the base matter to illuminate
> So vile a thing as Caesar! But, O grief,
> Where hast thou led me? I perhaps speak this
> Before a willing bondman. Then I know
> 115 My answer must be made. But I am armed,
> And dangers are to me indifferent.

CASCA

> You speak to Casca, and to such a man
> That is no fleering telltale. Hold, my hand.
> Be factious for redress of all these griefs,
> 120 And I will set this foot of mine as far
> As who goes farthest.

CASSIUS

> There's a bargain made.
> Now know you, Casca, I have moved already
> Some certain of the noblest-minded Romans
> To undergo with me an enterprise
> 125 Of honorable-dangerous consequence.
> And I do know by this they stay for me
> In Pompey's porch. For now, this fearful night,
> There is no stir or walking in the streets,
> And the complexion of the element
> 130 In favor's like the work we have in hand,
> Most bloody, fiery, and most terrible.

Enter CINNA

CASSIUS

How can Caesar be a tyrant then? Poor man! I know he wouldn't be a wolf if the Romans didn't act like sheep. He couldn't be a lion if the Romans weren't such easy prey. People who want to start a big fire quickly start with little twigs. Rome becomes complete trash, nothing but rubbish and garbage, when it works to light up the ambitions of someone as worthless as Caesar. But, oh no! What have I said in my grief? I might be speaking to someone who *wants* to be a slave, in which case I'll be held accountable for my words. But I'm armed and I don't care about danger.

CASCA

You're talking to Casca, not to some smiling, two-faced tattletale. Say no more. Shake my hand. If you're joining together to right these wrongs, I'll go as far as any one of you.

CASSIUS

That's a deal. Now let me tell you, Casca, I have already convinced some of the noblest Romans to join me in an honorable but dangerous mission. And I know that by now they're waiting for me on the porch outside Pompey's theater. We're meeting on this fearful night because no one is out on the streets. The sky tonight looks bloody, fiery, and terrible, just like the work we have to do.

CINNA *enters.*

CASCA
Stand close awhile, for here comes one in haste.

CASSIUS
'Tis Cinna. I do know him by his gait.
He is a friend.—Cinna, where haste you so?

CINNA
135   To find out you. Who's that? Metellus Cimber?

CASSIUS
No, it is Casca, one incorporate
To our attempts. Am I not stayed for, Cinna?

CINNA
I am glad on 't. What a fearful night is this!
There's two or three of us have seen strange sights.

CASSIUS
140   Am I not stayed for? Tell me.

CINNA
Yes, you are.
O Cassius, if you could
But win the noble Brutus to our party—

CASSIUS
Be you content. Good Cinna, take this paper,
145   And look you lay it in the praetor's chair
Where Brutus may but find it. And throw this
In at his window. Set this up with wax
Upon old Brutus' statue. All this done,
Repair to Pompey's porch, where you shall find us.
150   Is Decius Brutus and Trebonius there?

CINNA
All but Metellus Cimber, and he's gone
To seek you at your house. Well, I will hie,
And so bestow these papers as you bade me.

CASSIUS
That done, repair to Pompey's theatre.

Exit CINNA

CASCA

Hide for a minute—someone's approaching fast.

CASSIUS

It's Cinna. I recognize his walk. He's a friend. Cinna, where are you going in such a hurry?

CINNA

To find you. Who's that? Metellus Cimber?

CASSIUS

No, it's Casca, someone who's going to work with us. Aren't the others waiting for me, Cinna?

CINNA

I'm glad Casca is with us. What a fearful night this is! Two or three of us have seen strange things.

CASSIUS

Are the others waiting? Tell me.

CINNA

Yes, they are. Oh, Cassius, if you could only convince Brutus to join us—

CASSIUS

Don't worry. Good Cinna, take this paper and be sure to lay it in the judge's chair where Brutus sits, so he'll find it. And throw this one in his window, and attach this one with wax to the statue of Brutus's ancestor, old Brutus. When you've finished all this, return to the porch of Pompey's theater, where you'll find us. Are Decius Brutus and Trebonius there?

CINNA

Everyone's there except Metellus Cimber, and he's gone to look for you at your house. Well, I'll hurry and put these papers where you told me.

CASSIUS

When you've finished, go back to Pompey's theater.

CINNA exits.

155   Come, Casca, you and I will yet ere day
    See Brutus at his house. Three parts of him
    Is ours already, and the man entire
    Upon the next encounter yields him ours.

CASCA
    Oh, he sits high in all the people's hearts,
160   And that which would appear offense in us,
    His countenance, like richest alchemy,
    Will change to virtue and to worthiness.

CASSIUS
    Him and his worth and our great need of him
    You have right well conceited. Let us go,
165   For it is after midnight, and ere day
    We will awake him and be sure of him.

Exeunt

Come on, Casca, you and I will go see Brutus at his house before sunrise. He's three-quarters on our side already, and we'll win him over entirely at this meeting.

CASCA

Oh, the people love him well. Things that would look bad if we did them, Brutus could do and look virtuous—just like an alchemist turns worthless tin to gold.

CASSIUS

Yes, you're absolutely right about how worthy Brutus is and how much we need him. Let's go, because it's already after midnight, and we want him on our side before daylight.

They exit.

ACT TWO

SCENE 1

Enter BRUTUS *in his orchard*

BRUTUS
What, Lucius, ho!—
I cannot by the progress of the stars
Give guess how near to day.—Lucius, I say!—
I would it were my fault to sleep so soundly.—
5   When, Lucius, when? Awake, I say! What, Lucius!

Enter LUCIUS

LUCIUS
Called you, my lord?

BRUTUS
Get me a taper in my study, Lucius.
When it is lighted, come and call me here.

LUCIUS
I will, my lord.

Exit LUCIUS

BRUTUS
10   It must be by his death, and for my part
I know no personal cause to spurn at him
But for the general. He would be crowned.
How that might change his nature, there's the question.
It is the bright day that brings forth the adder
15   And that craves wary walking. Crown him that,
And then I grant we put a sting in him
That at his will he may do danger with.

ACT TWO
SCENE 1

BRUTUS *enters in his orchard.*

BRUTUS

Lucius, are you there? I can't tell by the position of the stars how near it is to daybreak—Lucius, are you there? I wish I had that weakness, to sleep too soundly. Come on, Lucius! Wake up, I say! Lucius!

LUCIUS *enters.*

LUCIUS

Did you call me, my lord?

BRUTUS

Put a candle in my study, Lucius. Call me when it's lit.

LUCIUS

I will, my lord.

LUCIUS *exits.*

BRUTUS

The only way is to kill Caesar. I have no personal reason to strike at him—only the best interest of the people. He wants to be crowned. The question is, how would being king change him? Evil can come from good, just as poisonous snakes tend to come out into the open on bright sunny days—which means we have to walk carefully. If we crown him, I have to admit we'd be giving him the power to do damage.

Th' abuse of greatness is when it disjoins
Remorse from power. And, to speak truth of Caesar,
20   I have not known when his affections swayed
More than his reason. But 'tis a common proof
That lowliness is young ambition's ladder,
Whereto the climber upward turns his face.
But when he once attains the upmost round,
25   He then unto the ladder turns his back,
Looks in the clouds, scorning the base degrees
By which he did ascend. So Caesar may.
Then, lest he may, prevent. And since the quarrel
Will bear no color for the thing he is,
30   Fashion it thus: that what he is, augmented,
Would run to these and these extremities.
And therefore think him as a serpent's egg—
Which, hatched, would as his kind grow mischievous—
And kill him in the shell.

Enter LUCIUS

LUCIUS
35   The taper burneth in your closet, sir.
Searching the window for a flint, I found
This paper, thus sealed up, and I am sure
It did not lie there when I went to bed.
(gives him a letter)

BRUTUS
Get you to bed again. It is not day.
40   Is not tomorrow, boy, the ides of March?
LUCIUS
I know not, sir.
BRUTUS
Look in the calendar and bring me word.
LUCIUS
I will, sir.

Rulers abuse their power when they separate it from compassion. To be honest, I've never known Caesar to let his emotions get the better of his reason. But everyone knows that an ambitious young man uses humility to advance himself, but when he reaches the top, he turns his back on his supporters and reaches for the skies while scorning those who helped him get where he is. Caesar might act like that. Therefore, in case he does, we must hold him back. And since our quarrel is with his future behavior, not what he does now, I must frame the argument like this: if his position is furthered, his character will fulfill these predictions. And therefore we should liken him to a serpent's egg—once it has hatched, it becomes dangerous, like all serpents. Thus we must kill him while he's still in the shell.

LUCIUS *enters.*

LUCIUS

The candle is burning in your study, sir. While I was looking for a flint to light it, I found this paper on the window, sealed up like this, and I'm sure it wasn't there when I went to bed. *(he gives* BRUTUS *the letter)*

BRUTUS

Go back to bed. It isn't daybreak yet. Is tomorrow the 15th of March, boy?

LUCIUS

I don't know, sir.

BRUTUS

Check the calendar and come tell me.

LUCIUS

I will, sir.

Exit LUCIUS

BRUTUS
        The exhalations whizzing in the air
45   Give so much light that I may read by them.
        (opens the letter and reads)
        "Brutus, thou sleep'st. Awake, and see thyself.
        Shall Rome, etc. Speak, strike, redress!"
        "Brutus, thou sleep'st. Awake."
        Such instigations have been often dropped
50   Where I have took them up.
        —"Shall Rome, etc." Thus must I piece it out:
        "Shall Rome stand under one man's awe?" What, Rome?
        My ancestors did from the streets of Rome
        The Tarquin drive when he was called a king.
55   —"Speak, strike, redress!" Am I entreated
        To speak and strike? O Rome, I make thee promise,
        If the redress will follow, thou receivest
        Thy full petition at the hand of Brutus!

        Enter LUCIUS

LUCIUS
        Sir, March is wasted fifteen days.

        Knock within

BRUTUS
60   'Tis good. Go to the gate. Somebody knocks.

Exit LUCIUS

        Since Cassius first did whet me against Caesar,
        I have not slept.

LUCIUS *exits.*

BRUTUS

The meteors whizzing in the sky are so bright that I can read by them. *(he opens the letter and reads)* "Brutus, you're sleeping. Wake up and look at yourself. Is Rome going to . . . etc. Speak, strike, fix the wrongs!" "Brutus, you're sleeping. Wake up." I've noticed many such calls to action left where I would find them. "Is Rome going to . . . etc." What does this mean? Will Rome submit to one man's power? My ancestors drove Tarquin from the streets of Rome when he was pronounced a king. "Speak, strike, fix it!" Is this asking me to speak and strike? Oh, Rome, I promise you, if you're meant to receive justice, you'll receive it by my hand!

LUCIUS *enters.*

LUCIUS

Sir, fifteen days of March have gone by.

The sound of a knock offstage.

BRUTUS

Good. Go to the gate. Somebody's knocking.

LUCIUS *exits.*

I haven't slept since Cassius first began to turn me against Caesar.

Between the acting of a dreadful thing
And the first motion, all the interim is
65   Like a phantasma or a hideous dream.
The genius and the mortal instruments
Are then in council, and the state of man,
Like to a little kingdom, suffers then
The nature of an insurrection.

Enter LUCIUS

LUCIUS
70   Sir, 'tis your brother Cassius at the door,
Who doth desire to see you.

BRUTUS
                                        Is he alone?

LUCIUS
No, sir, there are more with him.

BRUTUS
                                        Do you know them?

LUCIUS
No, sir. Their hats are plucked about their ears,
And half their faces buried in their cloaks,
75   That by no means I may discover them
By any mark of favor.

BRUTUS
                                        Let 'em enter.

Exit LUCIUS

They are the faction. O conspiracy,
Shamest thou to show thy dangerous brow by night
When evils are most free? O, then by day
80   Where wilt thou find a cavern dark enough
To mask thy monstrous visage? Seek none, conspiracy.
Hide it in smiles and affability.

From the time when you decide to do something terrible to the moment you do it, everything feels unreal,
like a horrible dream. The unconscious and the body
work together and rebel against the conscious mind.

LUCIUS *enters*.

LUCIUS

Sir, it's your brother-in-law Cassius at the door. He
wants to see you.

BRUTUS

Is he alone?

LUCIUS

No, sir. There are others with him.

BRUTUS

Do you know them?

LUCIUS

No, sir, their hats are pulled down over their ears and
their faces are half buried under their cloaks, so there's
no way to tell who they are.

BRUTUS

Let them in.

LUCIUS *exits*.

It's the faction that wants to kill Caesar. Oh, conspiracy, are you ashamed to show your face even at night,
when evil things are most free? If so, when it's day,
where are you going to find a cave dark enough to hide
your monstrous face? No, don't bother to find a cave,
conspiracy. Instead, hide your true face behind smiles
and friendliness.

For if thou path, thy native semblance on,
Not Erebus itself were dim enough
85   To hide thee from prevention.

Enter the conspirators: CASSIUS, CASCA, DECIUS, CINNA,
METELLUS, *and* TREBONIUS

CASSIUS
    I think we are too bold upon your rest.
    Good morrow, Brutus. Do we trouble you?

BRUTUS
    I have been up this hour, awake all night.
    Know I these men that come along with you?

CASSIUS
90   Yes, every man of them, and no man here
    But honors you, and every one doth wish
    You had but that opinion of yourself
    Which every noble Roman bears of you.
    This is Trebonius.

BRUTUS
                      He is welcome hither.

CASSIUS
95   This, Decius Brutus.

BRUTUS
    He is welcome too.

CASSIUS
    This, Casca. This, Cinna. And this, Metellus Cimber.

BRUTUS
    They are all welcome.
    What watchful cares do interpose themselves
100   Betwixt your eyes and night?

CASSIUS
    Shall I entreat a word?

    BRUTUS *and* CASSIUS *withdraw and whisper*

If you went ahead and exposed your true face, Hell itself wouldn't be dark enough to keep you from being found and stopped.

The conspirators—CASSIUS, CASCA, DECIUS, CINNA, METELLUS, *and* TREBONIUS—*enter.*

CASSIUS

I'm afraid we're intruding too boldly on your sleep time. Good morning, Brutus. Are we bothering you?

BRUTUS

I was awake. I've been up all night. Do I know these men who are with you?

CASSIUS

Yes, every one of them. There isn't one of them who doesn't admire you, and each one of them wishes you had as high an opinion of yourself as every noble Roman has of you. This is Trebonius.

BRUTUS

He's welcome here.

CASSIUS

This is Decius Brutus.

BRUTUS

He's welcome too.

CASSIUS

This is Casca. This is Cinna. And this is Metellus Cimber.

BRUTUS

They're all welcome. What worries have kept you awake tonight?

CASSIUS

Can I have a word with you?

BRUTUS *and* CASSIUS *whisper together.*

DECIUS
Here lies the east. Doth not the day break here?

CASCA
No.

CINNA
O, pardon, sir, it doth, and yon gray lines
105   That fret the clouds are messengers of day.

CASCA
You shall confess that you are both deceived.
(points his sword)
Here, as I point my sword, the sun arises,
Which is a great way growing on the south,
Weighing the youthful season of the year.
110   Some two months hence up higher toward the north
He first presents his fire, and the high east
Stands, as the Capitol, directly here.

BRUTUS
(comes forward with CASSIUS*)*
Give me your hands all over, one by one.
(shakes their hands)

CASSIUS
And let us swear our resolution.

BRUTUS
115   No, not an oath. If not the face of men,
The sufferance of our souls, the time's abuse—
If these be motives weak, break off betimes,
And every man hence to his idle bed.
So let high-sighted tyranny range on
120   Till each man drop by lottery. But if these—
As I am sure they do—bear fire enough
To kindle cowards and to steel with valor
The melting spirits of women, then, countrymen,
What need we any spur but our own cause
125   To prick us to redress? What other bond
Than secret Romans that have spoke the word

DECIUS

Here's the east. Won't the dawn come from here?

CASCA

No.

CINNA

Excuse me, sir, it will. These gray lines that lace the clouds are the beginnings of the dawn.

CASCA

You're both wrong. *(pointing his sword)* Here, where I point my sword, the sun rises. It's quite near the south, since it's still winter. About two months from now, the dawn will break further toward the north, and due east is where the Capitol stands, here.

BRUTUS

(coming forward with CASSIUS*)* Give me your hands, all of you, one by one. *(he shakes their hands)*

CASSIUS

And let us swear to our resolution.

BRUTUS

No, let's not swear an oath. If the sad faces of our fellow men, the suffering of our own souls, and the corruption of the present time aren't enough to motivate us, let's break it off now and each of us go back to bed. Then we can let this ambitious tyrant continue unchallenged until each of us is killed at his whim. But if we have reasons that are strong enough to ignite cowards into action and to make weak women brave— and I think we do—then, countrymen, what else could we possibly need to spur us to action? What bond do we need other than that of discreet Romans who have said what they're going to do and won't back down? And what oath do we need other than that we honest men have told each other that this will happen

And will not palter? And what other oath
Than honesty to honesty engaged,
That this shall be, or we will fall for it?
130 Swear priests and cowards and men cautelous,
Old feeble carrions and such suffering souls
That welcome wrongs. Unto bad causes swear
Such creatures as men doubt. But do not stain
The even virtue of our enterprise,
135 Nor th' insuppressive mettle of our spirits,
To think that or our cause or our performance
Did need an oath, when every drop of blood
That every Roman bears—and nobly bears—
Is guilty of a several bastardy
140 If he do break the smallest particle
Of any promise that hath passed from him.

CASSIUS
But what of Cicero? Shall we sound him?
I think he will stand very strong with us.

CASCA
Let us not leave him out.

CINNA
                                    No, by no means.

METELLUS
145 O, let us have him, for his silver hairs
Will purchase us a good opinion
And buy men's voices to commend our deeds.
It shall be said his judgment ruled our hands.
Our youths and wildness shall no whit appear,
150 But all be buried in his gravity.

BRUTUS
O, name him not. Let us not break with him,
For he will never follow anything
That other men begin.

CASSIUS
Then leave him out.

or we will die trying? Swearing is for priests, cowards, overly cautious men, feeble old people, and those long-suffering weaklings who welcome abuse. Only men whom you wouldn't trust anyway would swear oaths, and for the worst reasons. Don't spoil the justness and virtue of our endeavor nor weaken our own irrepressible spirits by thinking that we need a binding oath, when the blood that every noble Roman contains within him would be proven bastard's blood if he broke the smallest part of any promise he had made.

CASSIUS

But what about Cicero? Should we see what he thinks? I think he will stand strong with us.

CASCA

Let's not leave him out.

CINNA

No, by no means.

—blame Cicero

METELLUS

Yes, we should get his support, for his mature presence will make others think well of us and speak out in support of our actions. They'll assume that Cicero, with his sound judgment, ordered the actions. His dignified maturity will distract attention from our youth and wildness.

BRUTUS

No, don't even mention him. We shouldn't tell him about our plans. He'll never follow anything that other men have started.

CASSIUS

Then leave him out.

CASCA

Indeed, he's not right for this.

CASCA

155   Indeed he is not fit.

DECIUS

Shall no man else be touched but only Caesar?

CASSIUS

Decius, well urged. I think it is not meet
Mark Antony, so well beloved of Caesar,
Should outlive Caesar. We shall find of him
160   A shrewd contriver. And, you know, his means,
If he improve them, may well stretch so far
As to annoy us all; which to prevent,
Let Antony and Caesar fall together.

BRUTUS

Our course will seem too bloody, Caius Cassius,
165   To cut the head off and then hack the limbs,
Like wrath in death and envy afterwards,
For Antony is but a limb of Caesar.
Let us be sacrificers but not butchers, Caius.
We all stand up against the spirit of Caesar,
170   And in the spirit of men there is no blood.
Oh, that we then could come by Caesar's spirit
And not dismember Caesar! But, alas,
Caesar must bleed for it. And, gentle friends,
Let's kill him boldly but not wrathfully.
175   Let's carve him as a dish fit for the gods,
Not hew him as a carcass fit for hounds.
And let our hearts, as subtle masters do,
Stir up their servants to an act of rage
And after seem to chide 'em. This shall make
180   Our purpose necessary and not envious,
Which so appearing to the common eyes,
We shall be called purgers, not murderers.
And for Mark Antony, think not of him,
For he can do no more than Caesar's arm
185   When Caesar's head is off.

DECIUS

But should we only go after Caesar? No one else?

CASSIUS

Good point, Decius. I don't think it would be wise to let Mark Antony, whom Caesar is so fond of, outlive Caesar. We'd find that he was a dangerous plotter. And as you know, his connections, if he put them to good use, might be enough to hurt us all. To prevent this, Mark Antony should die along with Caesar.

BRUTUS

Our action will seem too bloody if we cut off Caesar's head and then hack at his arms and legs too, Caius Cassius—because Mark Antony is merely one of Caesar's arms. It'll look like we killed Caesar out of anger and Mark Antony out of envy. Let's be sacrificers but not butchers, Caius. We're all against what Caesar stands for, and there's no blood in that. Oh, how I wish we could oppose Caesar's spirit—his overblown ambition—and not hack up Caesar himself! But, unfortunately, Caesar has to bleed if we're going to stop him. Noble friends, let's kill him boldly but not with anger. Let's carve him up like a dish fit for the gods, not chop him up like a carcass fit for dogs. Let's be angry only long enough to do the deed, and then let's act like we're disgusted by what we had to do. This will make our actions seem practical and not vengeful. If we appear calm to the people, they'll call us surgeons rather than murderers. As for Mark Antony—forget him. He'll be as useless as Caesar's arm after Caesar's head is cut off.

CASSIUS

But I'm still afraid of him, because the deep-rooted love he has for Caesar—

CASSIUS

                                    Yet I fear him.
For in the engrafted love he bears to Caesar—

BRUTUS

Alas, good Cassius, do not think of him.
If he love Caesar, all that he can do
Is to himself: take thought and die for Caesar.
190   And that were much he should, for he is given
To sports, to wildness and much company.

TREBONIUS

There is no fear in him. Let him not die,
For he will live and laugh at this hereafter.

Clock strikes

BRUTUS

Peace! Count the clock.

CASSIUS

195   The clock hath stricken three.

TREBONIUS

'Tis time to part.

CASSIUS

                                    But it is doubtful yet
Whether Caesar will come forth today or no.
For he is superstitious grown of late,
Quite from the main opinion he held once
200   Of fantasy, of dreams and ceremonies.
It may be, these apparent prodigies,
The unaccustomed terror of this night,
And the persuasion of his augurers
May hold him from the Capitol today.

DECIUS

205   Never fear that. If he be so resolved,
I can o'ersway him. For he loves to hear
That unicorns may be betrayed with trees,
And bears with glasses, elephants with holes,

BRUTUS

Alas, good Cassius, don't think about him. If he loves Caesar, then he can only hurt himself—by grieving and dying for Caesar. And I'd be surprised if he even did that, for he prefers sports, fun, and friends.

TREBONIUS

There's nothing to fear in him. Let's not kill him. He'll live and laugh at this afterward.

A clock strikes.

BRUTUS

Quiet! Count how many times the clock chimes.

CASSIUS

The clock struck three.

TREBONIUS

It's time to leave.

CASSIUS

But we still don't know whether Caesar will go out in public today or not, because he's become superstitious lately, a complete turnaround from when he used to have such a bad opinion of fortune-tellers, dream interpreters, and ritual mumbo-jumbo. It might happen that these strange signs, the unusual terror of this night, and the urgings of his fortune-tellers will keep him away from the Capitol today.

DECIUS

Don't worry about that. If he's reluctant, I can convince him. He loves to hear me tell him how men can be snared by flatterers, just like unicorns can be captured in trees, elephants in holes, and lions with nets. When I tell him he hates flatterers, he agrees, just at the moment when I'm flattering him the most.

Lions with toils, and men with flatterers.
210 But when I tell him he hates flatterers,
He says he does, being then most flatterèd.
Let me work.
For I can give his humor the true bent,
And I will bring him to the Capitol.

CASSIUS
215 Nay, we will all of us be there to fetch him.

BRUTUS
By the eighth hour. Is that the uttermost?

CINNA
Be that the uttermost, and fail not then.

METELLUS
Caius Ligarius doth bear Caesar hard,
Who rated him for speaking well of Pompey.
220 I wonder none of you have thought of him.

BRUTUS
Now, good Metellus, go along by him.
He loves me well, and I have given him reasons.
Send him but hither and I'll fashion him.

CASSIUS
The morning comes upon 's. We'll leave you, Brutus.
225 —And, friends, disperse yourselves. But all remember
What you have said, and show yourselves true Romans.

BRUTUS
Good gentlemen, look fresh and merrily.
Let not our looks put on our purposes,
But bear it as our Roman actors do,
230 With untired spirits and formal constancy.
And so good morrow to you every one.

Exeunt. Manet **BRUTUS**

Let me work on him. I can put him in the right mood, and I'll bring him to the Capitol.

CASSIUS

No, we'll all go there to bring him.

BRUTUS

By eight o'clock. Is that the latest we can do it?

CINNA

Let's make that the latest, but be sure to get there before then.

METELLUS

Caius Ligarius doesn't like Caesar, who berated him for speaking well of Pompey. I wonder that none of you thought about getting his support.

BRUTUS

Good Metellus, go to him now. He likes me, and I've given him good reason to. Just send him here, and I'll persuade him.

CASSIUS

The morning is approaching. We'll leave, Brutus. Friends, go your separate ways. But all of you, remember what you've said and prove yourselves true Romans.

BRUTUS

Good gentlemen, look like you're rested and happy. Don't let our faces betray our plans. Instead, carry yourselves like Roman actors, with cheerful spirits and well-composed faces. And so, good morning to all of you.

Everyone except BRUTUS *exits.*

Boy! Lucius!—Fast asleep? It is no matter.
Enjoy the honey-heavy dew of slumber.
Thou hast no figures nor no fantasies,
235   Which busy care draws in the brains of men.
Therefore thou sleep'st so sound.

Enter PORTIA

PORTIA

                                    Brutus, my lord.
BRUTUS
Portia, what mean you? Wherefore rise you now?
It is not for your health thus to commit
Your weak condition to the raw, cold morning.
PORTIA
240   Nor for yours neither. Y' have ungently, Brutus,
Stole from my bed. And yesternight, at supper,
You suddenly arose and walked about,
Musing and sighing, with your arms across,
And when I asked you what the matter was,
245   You stared upon me with ungentle looks.
I urged you further, then you scratched your head
And too impatiently stamped with your foot.
Yet I insisted; yet you answered not,
But with an angry wafture of your hand
250   Gave sign for me to leave you. So I did,
Fearing to strengthen that impatience
Which seemed too much enkindled, and withal
Hoping it was but an effect of humor,
Which sometime hath his hour with every man.
255   It will not let you eat nor talk nor sleep,
And could it work so much upon your shape
As it hath much prevailed on your condition,
I should not know you, Brutus. Dear my lord,
Make me acquainted with your cause of grief.

Boy! Lucius! Fast asleep? Well, enjoy the sweetness of deep sleep. Your brain isn't stuffed with the strange shapes and fantasies that come to men who are overwhelmed by worries. That's why you sleep so soundly.

PORTIA *enters.*

PORTIA

Brutus, my lord.

BRUTUS

Portia, what are you doing awake? It isn't good for your health to expose your weak body to the raw, cold morning.

PORTIA

It's not good for your health, either. You rudely snuck out of bed. And last night at dinner, you got up abruptly and paced back and forth with your arms crossed, brooding and sighing, and when I asked you what was the matter, you gave me a dirty look. I asked you again, and you scratched your head and stamped your foot impatiently. I still insisted on knowing what the matter was, but you wouldn't answer me, instead giving me an angry wave of your hand and telling me to leave you alone. So I left, afraid of further provoking anger that was already inflamed but still hoping this was merely moodiness, which everyone is affected by once in awhile. Your strange mood won't let you eat or talk or sleep. If it had changed your outward appearance as much as it has affected you on the inside, I wouldn't even be able to recognize you, Brutus. My dear lord, tell me what's bothering you.

BRUTUS

260   I am not well in health, and that is all.

PORTIA

     Brutus is wise, and were he not in health,
     He would embrace the means to come by it.

BRUTUS

     Why, so I do. Good Portia, go to bed.

PORTIA

     Is Brutus sick? And is it physical
265   To walk unbracèd and suck up the humors
     Of the dank morning? What, is Brutus sick,
     And will he steal out of his wholesome bed,
     To dare the vile contagion of the night
     And tempt the rheumy and unpurgèd air
270   To add unto his sickness? No, my Brutus.
     You have some sick offense within your mind,
     Which by the right and virtue of my place
     I ought to know of. *(kneels)* And upon my knees
     I charm you, by my once-commended beauty,
275   By all your vows of love and that great vow
     Which did incorporate and make us one
     That you unfold to me, your self, your half,
     Why you are heavy, and what men tonight
     Have had to resort to you. For here have been
280   Some six or seven who did hide their faces
     Even from darkness.

BRUTUS

                    Kneel not, gentle Portia.

PORTIA

     (rising) I should not need if you were gentle, Brutus.
     Within the bond of marriage, tell me, Brutus,
     Is it excepted I should know no secrets
     That appertain to you? Am I yourself
285   But, as it were, in sort or limitation,
     To keep with you at meals, comfort your bed,
     And talk to you sometimes?

BRUTUS

I'm not feeling well—that's all.

PORTIA

You're smart, though, and if you were sick, you'd take what you needed to get better.

BRUTUS

I'm doing so. Good Portia, go to bed.

PORTIA

Are you sick? And is it healthy to walk uncovered and breathe in the dampness of the morning? You're sick, yet you sneak out of your warm bed and let the humid and disease-infested air make you sicker? No, my Brutus, you have some sickness within your mind, which by virtue of my position I deserve to know about. *(she kneels)* And on my knees, I urge you, by my once-praised beauty, by all your vows of love and that great vow of marriage which made the two of us one person, that you should reveal to me, who is one half of yourself, why you're troubled and what men have visited you tonight. For there were six or seven men here, who hid their faces even in the darkness.

BRUTUS

Don't kneel, noble Portia.

PORTIA

(getting up) I wouldn't need to if you were acting nobly. Tell me, Brutus, as your wife, aren't I supposed to be told the secrets that concern you? Am I part of you only in a limited sense—I get to have dinner with you, sleep with you, and talk to you sometimes?

                                Dwell I but in the suburbs
Of your good pleasure? If it be no more,
Portia is Brutus' harlot, not his wife.

BRUTUS

290   You are my true and honorable wife,
As dear to me as are the ruddy drops
That visit my sad heart.

PORTIA

If this were true, then should I know this secret.
I grant I am a woman, but withal
295   A woman that Lord Brutus took to wife.
I grant I am a woman, but withal
A woman well-reputed, Cato's daughter.
Think you I am no stronger than my sex,
Being so fathered and so husbanded?
300   Tell me your counsels. I will not disclose 'em.
I have made strong proof of my constancy,
Giving myself a voluntary wound
Here in the thigh. Can I bear that with patience,
And not my husband's secrets?

BRUTUS

                                O ye gods,
305   Render me worthy of this noble wife!

Knock within

Hark, hark! One knocks. Portia, go in awhile.
And by and by thy bosom shall partake
The secrets of my heart.
All my engagements I will construe to thee,
310   All the charactery of my sad brows.
Leave me with haste.

                                Exit **PORTIA**

Lucius, who's that knocks?

Is my place only on the outskirts of your happiness? If it's nothing more than that, then I'm your whore, not your wife.

161

BRUTUS

You're my true and honorable wife, as dear to me as the blood that runs through my sad heart.

PORTIA

If that were true, then I'd know your secret. I admit I'm only a woman, but nevertheless I'm the woman Lord Brutus took for his wife. I admit I'm only a woman, but I'm still a woman from a noble family— I'm Cato's daughter. Do you really think I'm no stronger than the rest of my sex, with such a father and such a husband? Tell me your secrets. I won't betray them. I've proved my trustworthiness by giving myself a voluntary wound here in my thigh. If I can bear that pain, then I can bear my husband's secrets.

BRUTUS

Oh, gods, make me worthy of this noble wife!

A knocking sound offstage.

Listen! Someone knocks. Portia, go inside awhile, and soon enough you'll share the secrets of my heart. I'll explain all that I have committed to do and all the reasons for my sad face. Leave me quickly.

PORTIA *exits.*

Lucius, who's that knocking?

Enter LUCIUS *and* LIGARIUS

LUCIUS
He is a sick man that would speak with you.

BRUTUS
Caius Ligarius, that Metellus spake of.—
315   Boy, stand aside.—Caius Ligarius, how?

LIGARIUS
Vouchsafe good morrow from a feeble tongue.

BRUTUS
O, what a time have you chose out, brave Caius,
To wear a kerchief! Would you were not sick!

LIGARIUS
I am not sick if Brutus have in hand
320   Any exploit worthy the name of honor.

BRUTUS
Such an exploit have I in hand, Ligarius,
Had you a healthful ear to hear of it.

LIGARIUS
(removes his kerchief)
By all the gods that Romans bow before,
I here discard my sickness! Soul of Rome,
325   Brave son derived from honorable loins,
Thou, like an exorcist, hast conjurèd up
My mortifièd spirit. Now bid me run,
And I will strive with things impossible,
Yea, get the better of them. What's to do?

BRUTUS
330   A piece of work that will make sick men whole.

LIGARIUS
But are not some whole that we must make sick?

BRUTUS
That must we also. What it is, my Caius,
I shall unfold to thee as we are going
To whom it must be done.

LUCIUS and LIGARIUS enter. Ligarius wears a cloth wrapped around his head, indicating that he's sick.

LUCIUS

Here's a sick man who wants to speak with you.

BRUTUS

It's Caius Ligarius, whom Metellus spoke of. Boy, stand aside. Caius Ligarius! How are you?

LIGARIUS

Please accept my feeble "good morning."

BRUTUS

Oh, what a time you've chosen to be sick, brave Caius! How I wish you felt better!

LIGARIUS

I'm not sick if you've prepared some honorable exploit for me.

BRUTUS

Indeed, I would have such an exploit for you, Ligarius, if you were healthy enough to hear it.

LIGARIUS

(takes off his head covering) By all the gods that Romans worship, I hereby throw off my sickness! Soul of Rome! Brave son of honorable ancestors! You've conjured up my deadened spirit like an exorcist. Now say the word, and I will tackle all kinds of impossible things, and succeed too. What is there to do?

BRUTUS

A deed that will make sick men healthy.

LIGARIUS

But aren't there some healthy men whom we have to make sick?

BRUTUS

That too. My dear Caius, I'll explain the task at hand to you as we walk toward the man we must do it to.

LIGARIUS
                              Set on your foot,
335   And with a heart new-fired I follow you,
      To do I know not what. But it sufficeth
      That Brutus leads me on.

      Thunder

BRUTUS
                              Follow me, then.
                                              Exeunt

LIGARIUS

Start walking, and with an energized heart, I'll follow you—to what, I don't know, but I'm satisfied, simply knowing that Brutus leads me.

Thunder.

BRUTUS

Follow me, then.

They all exit.

ACT 2, SCENE 2

Thunder and lightning
Enter Julius CAESAR *in his nightgown*

CAESAR

Nor heaven nor earth have been at peace tonight.
Thrice hath Calphurnia in her sleep cried out,
"Help, ho! They murder Caesar!"—Who's within?

Enter a SERVANT

SERVANT

My lord.

CAESAR

5   Go bid the priests do present sacrifice
And bring me their opinions of success.

SERVANT

I will, my lord.

Exit SERVANT

Enter CALPHURNIA

CALPHURNIA

What mean you, Caesar? Think you to walk forth?
You shall not stir out of your house today.

CAESAR

10   Caesar shall forth. The things that threatened me
Ne'er looked but on my back. When they shall see
The face of Caesar, they are vanishèd.

CALPHURNIA

Caesar, I never stood on ceremonies,
Yet now they fright me. There is one within,
15   Besides the things that we have heard and seen,
Recounts most horrid sights seen by the watch.
A lioness hath whelpèd in the streets,
And graves have yawned and yielded up their dead.

ACT 2, SCENE 2

Thunder and lightning. CAESAR *enters in his nightgown.*

CAESAR

Neither the sky nor the earth have been quiet tonight. Calphurnia cried out three times in her sleep, "Help, someone! They're murdering Caesar!" Who's there?

A SERVANT *enters.*

SERVANT

My lord?

CAESAR

Go tell the priests to perform a sacrifice immediately, and bring me their interpretation of the results.

SERVANT

I will, my lord.

The SERVANT *exits.*

CALPHURNIA *enters.*

CALPHURNIA

What are you doing, Caesar? Are you planning to go out? You're not leaving the house today.

CAESAR

I will go out. The things that threaten me have only seen my back. When they see the face of Caesar, they will vanish.

CALPHURNIA

Caesar, I never believed in omens, but now they frighten me. A servant told me the night-watchmen saw horrid sights too, but different ones from what we heard and saw. A lioness gave birth in the streets, and graves cracked open and thrust out their dead.

be scared Caesar

what

        Fierce fiery warriors fought upon the clouds
20   In ranks and squadrons and right form of war,
        Which drizzled blood upon the Capitol.
        The noise of battle hurtled in the air.
        Horses did neigh, and dying men did groan,
        And ghosts did shriek and squeal about the streets.
25   O Caesar! These things are beyond all use,
        And I do fear them.

CAESAR
                    What can be avoided
        Whose end is purposed by the mighty gods?
        Yet Caesar shall go forth, for these predictions
        Are to the world in general as to Caesar.

CALPHURNIA
30   When beggars die there are no comets seen.
        The heavens themselves blaze forth the death of princes.

CAESAR
        Cowards die many times before their deaths.
        The valiant never taste of death but once.
        Of all the wonders that I yet have heard,
35   It seems to me most strange that men should fear,
        Seeing that death, a necessary end,
        Will come when it will come.

        Enter SERVANT

                    What say the augurers?

SERVANT
        They would not have you to stir forth today.
        Plucking the entrails of an offering forth,
40   They could not find a heart within the beast.

CAESAR
        The gods do this in shame of cowardice.
        Caesar should be a beast without a heart
        If he should stay at home today for fear.
        No, Caesar shall not. Danger knows full well

Fierce, fiery warriors fought in the clouds in the usual formations of war—ranks and squadrons—until the clouds drizzled blood onto the Capitol. The noise of battle filled the air, and horses neighed, and dying men groaned, and ghosts shrieked and squealed in the streets. Oh, Caesar! These things are beyond anything we've seen before, and I'm afraid.

CAESAR

How can we avoid what the gods want to happen? But I will go out, for these bad omens apply to the world in general as much as they do to me.

CALPHURNIA

When beggars die there are no comets in the sky. The heavens only announce the deaths of princes.

CAESAR

Cowards die many times before their deaths. The brave experience death only once. Of all the strange things I've ever heard, it seems most strange to me that men fear death, given that death, which can't be avoided, will come whenever it wants.

The SERVANT *enters.*

What do the priests say?

SERVANT

They don't want you to go out today. They pulled out the guts of the sacrificed animal and couldn't find its heart.

CAESAR

The gods do this to test my bravery. They're saying I'd be an animal without a heart if I stayed home today out of fear. So, I won't.

↳ fearless

45 That Caesar is more dangerous than he.
We are two lions littered in one day,
And I the elder and more terrible.
And Caesar shall go forth.

CALPHURNIA

                            Alas, my lord,
Your wisdom is consumed in confidence.
50 Do not go forth today. Call it my fear
That keeps you in the house, and not your own.
We'll send Mark Antony to the senate house,
And he shall say you are not well today.
(kneels) Let me, upon my knee, prevail in this.

CAESAR

55 Mark Antony shall say I am not well,
And for thy humor I will stay at home.

CALPHURNIA *rises*
Enter DECIUS

Here's Decius Brutus. He shall tell them so.

DECIUS

Caesar, all hail! Good morrow, worthy Caesar.
I come to fetch you to the senate house.

CAESAR

60 And you are come in very happy time
To bear my greeting to the senators
And tell them that I will not come today.
"Cannot" is false, and that I dare not, falser.
I will not come today. Tell them so, Decius.

CALPHURNIA

65 Say he is sick.

CAESAR

                    Shall Caesar send a lie?
Have I in conquest stretched mine arm so far
To be afraid to tell graybeards the truth?

Danger knows that Caesar is more dangerous than he is. We're two lions born on the same day in the same litter, and I'm the older and more terrible. I will go out.

CALPHURNIA

Alas, my lord, your confidence is getting the better of your wisdom. Don't go out today. Say that it's my fear that keeps you inside and not your own. We'll send Mark Antony to the senate house, and he'll say that you're sick today. *(she kneels)* Let me, on my knees, win you over to this plan.

CAESAR

All right. Mark Antony will say I'm not well, and to please you I'll stay at home.

CALPHURNIA *gets up.*
DECIUS *enters.*

Here's Decius Brutus. He'll tell them so.

DECIUS

Hail, Caesar! Good morning, worthy Caesar. I've come to take you to the senate house.

CAESAR

And you've come at a good time, so you can convey my greetings to the senators and tell them I won't come today. It wouldn't be true to say that I *can't* come, and even less true to say that I don't *dare* come. I simply *won't* come today. Tell them so, Decius.

CALPHURNIA

Say he's sick.

CAESAR

Would I send a lie? Have I accomplished so much in battle, but now I'm afraid to tell some old men the truth?

Decius, go tell them Caesar will not come.

DECIUS

Most mighty Caesar, let me know some cause,
70   Lest I be laughed at when I tell them so.

CAESAR

The cause is in my will. I will not come.
That is enough to satisfy the senate.
But for your private satisfaction,
Because I love you, I will let you know.
75   Calphurnia here, my wife, stays me at home.
She dreamt tonight she saw my statue,
Which, like a fountain with an hundred spouts,
Did run pure blood. And many lusty Romans
Came smiling and did bathe their hands in it.
80   And these does she apply for warnings and portents
And evils imminent, and on her knee
Hath begged that I will stay at home today.

DECIUS

This dream is all amiss interpreted.
It was a vision fair and fortunate.
85   Your statue spouting blood in many pipes,
In which so many smiling Romans bathed,
Signifies that from you great Rome shall suck
Reviving blood, and that great men shall press
For tinctures, stains, relics, and cognizance.
90   This by Calphurnia's dream is signified.

CAESAR

And this way have you well expounded it.

DECIUS

I have, when you have heard what I can say.
And know it now: the senate have concluded
To give this day a crown to mighty Caesar.

Decius, go tell them that Caesar won't come.

DECIUS

Most mighty Caesar, give me some reason, so I won't be laughed at when I tell them so.

CAESAR

The reason is that it's what I want. I'm not coming. That's enough for the senate. But for your private satisfaction, because I love you, I'll tell you. Calphurnia, my wife, is keeping me at home. Last night, she dreamed she saw a statue of me with a hundred holes in it, like a fountain with pure blood flowing from it, and many happy Romans came smiling and washed their hands in it. She takes these signs for warnings and predictions of terrible evils to come, and, on her knee, she begged me to stay home today.

trying to get him to go

DECIUS

This dream has been interpreted all wrong. It was a good and lucky vision. Your statue spouting blood through many holes, in which many smiling Romans bathed, means that you'll provide great Rome with sustaining blood, and that great men will strive to get some token of approval from your holy blood. This is what Calphurnia's dream means.

CAESAR

You've offered an excellent interpretation.

HA!

DECIUS

I will have when you hear the rest of what I have to say. The senate has decided to give mighty Caesar a crown today.

95   If you shall send them word you will not come,
      Their minds may change. Besides, it were a mock
      Apt to be rendered for someone to say,
      "Break up the senate till another time
      When Caesar's wife shall meet with better dreams."
100   If Caesar hide himself, shall they not whisper,
      "Lo, Caesar is afraid"?
      Pardon me, Caesar. For my dear, dear love
      To your proceeding bids me tell you this,
      And reason to my love is liable.

CAESAR
105   How foolish do your fears seem now, Calphurnia!
      I am ashamèd I did yield to them.
      Give me my robe, for I will go.

Enter BRUTUS, LIGARIUS, METELLUS, CASCA, TREBONIUS,
CINNA, *and* PUBLIUS

      And look, where Publius is come to fetch me.

PUBLIUS
      Good morrow, Caesar.

CAESAR
110   Welcome, Publius.
      —What, Brutus, are you stirred so early too?
      —Good morrow, Casca.—Caius Ligarius,
      Caesar was ne'er so much your enemy
      As that same ague which hath made you lean.
115   —What is 't o'clock?

BRUTUS
                              Caesar, 'tis strucken eight.

CAESAR
      I thank you for your pains and courtesy.

Enter ANTONY

If you send them word that you won't come, they might change their minds. Besides, someone's likely to joke, "Adjourn the senate until some other time, when Caesar's wife has had better dreams." If you hide yourself, won't they whisper, "Caesar is afraid?" Pardon me, Caesar. My high hopes for your advancement force me to tell you this. My love gets the better of my manners.

CAESAR

How foolish your fears seem now, Calphurnia! I'm ashamed that I yielded to them. Give me my robe, because I'm going.

PUBLIUS, BRUTUS, LIGARIUS, METELLUS, CASCA, TREBONIUS, *and* CINNA *enter.*

And look, here's Publius, come to fetch me.

PUBLIUS

Good morning, Caesar.

CAESAR

Welcome, Publius. What, Brutus? Are you up this early too? Good morning, Casca. Caius Ligarius, I was never your enemy so much as the sickness that's made you so thin. What time is it?

BRUTUS

Caesar, the clock has struck eight.

CAESAR

I thank you all for your trouble and courtesy.

ANTONY *enters.*

See, Antony, that revels long a-nights,
Is notwithstanding up.—Good morrow, Antony.

ANTONY
So to most noble Caesar.

CAESAR
                                        Bid them prepare within.
120   I am to blame to be thus waited for.
—Now, Cinna.—Now, Metellus.—What, Trebonius,
I have an hour's talk in store for you.
Remember that you call on me today.
Be near me, that I may remember you.

TREBONIUS
125   Caesar, I will. *(aside)* And so near will I be
That your best friends shall wish I had been further.

CAESAR
Good friends, go in and taste some wine with me.
And we, like friends, will straightway go together.

BRUTUS
(aside) That every "like" is not the same, O Caesar,
130   The heart of Brutus earns to think upon.

Exeunt

See! Even Antony, who stays up all night partying, is awake. Good morning, Antony.

ANTONY

And to you, most noble Caesar.

CAESAR

Tell them to prepare the other room for guests. I'm to blame for making you wait for me. Now, Cinna. Now, Metellus. Trebonius! I have an hour-long matter to discuss with you. Remember to see me today. Stay near me so I'll remember.

TREBONIUS

Caesar, I will. *(speaking quietly to himself)* In fact, I'll be so near that your best friends will wish I'd been further away.

CAESAR

Good friends, go in and have some wine with me. And we'll leave together, like friends.

BRUTUS

(quietly to himself) That we are now only "like" friends—Oh Caesar—makes my heart ache.

They all exit.

ACT 2, SCENE 3

Enter ARTEMIDORUS, *reading a letter*

ARTEMIDORUS
    (reads aloud)
        "Caesar, beware of Brutus. Take heed of Cassius.
        Come not near Casca. Have an eye to Cinna. Trust not
        Trebonius. Mark well Metellus Cimber. Decius
        Brutus loves thee not. Thou hast wronged Caius
5   Ligarius. There is but one mind in all these men, and
        it is bent against Caesar. If thou beest not immortal,
        look about you. Security gives way to conspiracy. The
        mighty gods defend thee!
                        Thy lover,
                        Artemidorus"
    Here will I stand till Caesar pass along,
10   And as a suitor will I give him this.
    My heart laments that virtue cannot live
    Out of the teeth of emulation.
    If thou read this, O Caesar, thou mayst live.
    If not, the Fates with traitors do contrive.

                                    Exit

ACT 2, SCENE 3

ARTEMIDORUS *enters, reading a letter.*

ARTEMIDORUS

(reading aloud from the letter)

"Caesar, beware of Brutus. Watch Cassius. Don't go near Casca. Keep an eye on Cinna. Don't trust Trebonius. Pay attention to Metellus Cimber. Decius Brutus doesn't love you. You've wronged Caius Ligarius. These men all have one intention, and it's directed against Caesar. If you aren't immortal, watch those around you. A sense of security opens the door to conspiracy. I pray that the mighty gods defend you!

Your friend,
Artemidorus."

I'll stand here until Caesar passes by, and I'll give him this as though it's a petition. My heart regrets that good men aren't safe from the bite of jealous rivals. If you read this, Caesar, you might live. If not, the Fates are on the side of the traitors.

He exits.

ACT 2, SCENE 4

Enter PORTIA *and* LUCIUS

PORTIA
> I prithee, boy, run to the senate house.
> Stay not to answer me, but get thee gone.
> Why dost thou stay?

LUCIUS
> To know my errand, madam.

PORTIA
> I would have had thee there and here again
> 5   Ere I can tell thee what thou shouldst do there.
> —O constancy, be strong upon my side,
> Set a huge mountain 'tween my heart and tongue!
> I have a man's mind but a woman's might.
> How hard it is for women to keep counsel!
> 10   —Art thou here yet?

LUCIUS
> Madam, what should I do?
> Run to the Capitol, and nothing else?
> And so return to you, and nothing else?

PORTIA
> Yes, bring me word, boy, if thy lord look well,
> For he went sickly forth. And take good note
> 15   What Caesar doth, what suitors press to him.
> Hark, boy! What noise is that?

LUCIUS
> I hear none, madam.

PORTIA
> Prithee, listen well.
> I heard a bustling rumor like a fray,
> 20   And the wind brings it from the Capitol.

LUCIUS
> Sooth, madam, I hear nothing.

Enter the SOOTHSAYER

ACT 2, SCENE 4

PORTIA and LUCIUS enter.

PORTIA

Boy, I beg you to run to the senate house. Don't stay to answer me—get going. Why are you still standing there?

LUCIUS

To find out what you want me to do there, madam.

PORTIA

I want you there and back again before I can even tell you what you should do there. *(to herself, so that no one can hear her)* Oh, let my determination keep me from speaking what is in my heart! I have a man's mind, but only a woman's strength. How hard it is for women to keep secrets! *(to LUCIUS)* Are you still here?

LUCIUS

Madam, what should I do? Run to the Capitol and nothing else? And then return to you and nothing else?

PORTIA

Yes, return and tell me if your master looks well, because he was sick when he left. And pay attention to what Caesar does and which men are close to him. Listen, boy! What's that noise?

LUCIUS

I don't hear anything, madam.

PORTIA

I beg you, listen well. I heard a noise like a scuffle. The wind brings it from the Capitol.

LUCIUS

Truly, madam, I don't hear anything.

The SOOTHSAYER enters.

PORTIA
> Come hither, fellow. Which way hast thou been?

SOOTHSAYER
> At mine own house, good lady.

PORTIA
> What is 't o'clock?

SOOTHSAYER
25 > About the ninth hour, lady.

PORTIA
> Is Caesar yet gone to the Capitol?

SOOTHSAYER
> Madam, not yet. I go to take my stand
> To see him pass on to the Capitol.

PORTIA
> Thou hast some suit to Caesar, hast thou not?

SOOTHSAYER
30 > That I have, lady. If it will please Caesar
> To be so good to Caesar as to hear me,
> I shall beseech him to befriend himself.

PORTIA
> Why, know'st thou any harm's intended towards him?

SOOTHSAYER
> None that I know will be; much that I fear may chance.
35 > Good morrow to you. Here the street is narrow.
> The throng that follows Caesar at the heels,
> Of senators, of praetors, common suitors,
> Will crowd a feeble man almost to death.
> I'll get me to a place more void, and there
40 > Speak to great Caesar as he comes along.

Exit SOOTHSAYER

PORTIA

Come here, you. Where are you coming from?

SOOTHSAYER

My own house, good lady.

PORTIA

What time is it?

SOOTHSAYER

Around nine o'clock, madam.

PORTIA

Has Caesar gone to the Capitol yet?

SOOTHSAYER

Madam, not yet. I'm going to stand so I can see him pass on the way to the Capitol.

PORTIA

You have some plea for Caesar, don't you?

SOOTHSAYER

Yes, I do, lady. If it pleases Caesar to be so good to himself as to hear me, I'll try to get him to do what's good for him.

PORTIA

Why, do you know of any harm intended toward him?

SOOTHSAYER

Nothing that I know for sure, but a lot that I'm afraid might happen. Good morning to you. The street is narrow here. The crowd that follows Caesar at his heels—senators, justices, common petitioners—will suffocate a feeble man almost to death. I'll move to a more open place and there speak to great Caesar as he walks past.

He exits.

PORTIA
I must go in. *(aside)* Ay me, how weak a thing
The heart of woman is! O Brutus,
The heavens speed thee in thine enterprise!
Sure, the boy heard me. *(to* LUCIUS*)* Brutus hath a suit
45　That Caesar will not grant.—Oh, I grow faint.—
Run, Lucius, and commend me to my lord.
Say I am merry. Come to me again,
And bring me word what he doth say to thee.

Exeunt severally

PORTIA

I must go in. *(speaking quietly to herself)* Oh, a woman's heart is so weak! Oh Brutus, may the gods aid you in your endeavor! Surely, the boy heard me. *(to* LUCIUS*)* Brutus has a claim that Caesar won't grant. Oh, I feel faint. Run, Lucius, and speak well of me to my lord. Say that I'm happy. Then return to me and tell me what he says to you.

They exit in opposite directions.

ACT THREE
SCENE 1

Flourish
Enter CAESAR, BRUTUS, CASSIUS, CASCA, DECIUS, METELLUS,
TREBONIUS, CINNA, ANTONY, LEPIDUS, PUBLIUS, *and*
POPILLIUS LENA *with a crowd of people, including*
ARTEMIDORUS *and the* SOOTHSAYER

CAESAR
(to the SOOTHSAYER*)* The ides of March are come.

SOOTHSAYER
Ay, Caesar, but not gone.

ARTEMIDORUS
(offering his letter) Hail, Caesar! Read this schedule.

DECIUS
(offering CAESAR *another paper)*
Trebonius doth desire you to o'er-read,
5   At your best leisure, this his humble suit.

ARTEMIDORUS
O Caesar, read mine first, for mine's a suit
That touches Caesar nearer. Read it, great Caesar.

CAESAR
What touches us ourself shall be last served.

ARTEMIDORUS
Delay not, Caesar. Read it instantly.

CAESAR
10   What, is the fellow mad?

PUBLIUS
(to ARTEMIDORUS*)*   Sirrah, give place.

CASSIUS
(to ARTEMIDORUS*)*
What, urge you your petitions in the street?
Come to the Capitol.

ACT THREE
SCENE 1

A crowd of people enters, among them ARTEMIDORUS *and the* SOOTHSAYER. *A trumpet plays.* CAESAR, BRUTUS, CASSIUS, CASCA, DECIUS, METELLUS, TREBONIUS, CINNA, ANTONY, LEPIDUS, POPILLIUS, PUBLIUS, *and others enter.*

CAESAR

(to the SOOTHSAYER*)* March 15th has come.

SOOTHSAYER

Yes, Caesar, but it's not gone yet.

ARTEMIDORUS

(offering his letter) Hail, Caesar! Read this schedule.

DECIUS

(offering CAESAR *another paper)* Trebonius wants you to look over his humble petition, at your leisure.

ARTEMIDORUS

Oh, Caesar, read mine first, for my petition affects you more directly. Read it, great Caesar.

CAESAR

Whatever pertains to myself I will deal with last. — numb?

ARTEMIDORUS

Don't delay, Caesar. Read it instantly.

CAESAR

What, is the man insane?

PUBLIUS

(to ARTEMIDORUS*)* Stand aside, you.

CASSIUS

(to ARTEMIDORUS*)* What? Are you pressing your petition on the street? Go to the Capitol.

CAESAR's party moves aside to the senate house

POPILLIUS
    (to CASSIUS) I wish your enterprise today may thrive.

CASSIUS
    What enterprise, Popillius?

POPILLIUS
                         Fare you well.

    (approaches CAESAR)

BRUTUS
15   *(to CASSIUS)* What said Popillius Lena?

CASSIUS
    (aside to BRUTUS)
    He wished today our enterprise might thrive.
    I fear our purpose is discoverèd.

BRUTUS
    Look how he makes to Caesar. Mark him.

CASSIUS
    Casca, be sudden, for we fear prevention
20   —Brutus, what shall be done? If this be known,
    Cassius or Caesar never shall turn back,
    For I will slay myself.

BRUTUS
                  Cassius, be constant.
    Popillius Lena speaks not of our purposes.
    For, look, he smiles, and Caesar doth not change.

CASSIUS
25   Trebonius knows his time. For, look you, Brutus.
    He draws Mark Antony out of the way.

    Exeunt TREBONIUS and ANTONY

DECIUS
    Where is Metellus Cimber? Let him go
    And presently prefer his suit to Caesar.

CAESAR *goes up to the senate house, the rest following.*

POPILLIUS

(to CASSIUS) I hope your endeavor goes well today.

CASSIUS

What endeavor, Popillius?

POPILLIUS

Good luck.

POPILLIUS *approaches* CAESAR.

BRUTUS

(to CASSIUS) What did Popillius Lena say?

CASSIUS

(speaking so that only BRUTUS can hear) He wished that our endeavor would go well today. I'm afraid we've been found out.

BRUTUS

Look, he's approaching Caesar. Keep an eye on him.

CASSIUS

Casca, be quick, because we're worried we might be stopped. Brutus, what will we do? If our secret's known, either Caesar or I will die, for I'll kill myself.

BRUTUS

Cassius, stand firm. Popillius Lena wasn't talking about our plot—for, look, he's smiling, and Caesar's expression is the same.

CASSIUS

Trebonius knows his cue. See, Brutus, he's pulling Mark Antony aside.

TREBONIUS *and* ANTONY *exit.*

DECIUS

Where's Metellus Cimber? He should go up and offer his petition to Caesar now.

BRUTUS
He is addressed. Press near and second him.

CINNA
30   Casca, you are the first that rears your hand.

CAESAR
Are we all ready? What is now amiss
That Caesar and his senate must redress?

METELLUS
(kneeling)
Most high, most mighty, and most puissant Caesar,
Metellus Cimber throws before thy seat
35   An humble heart—

CAESAR
                              I must prevent thee, Cimber.
These couchings and these lowly courtesies
Might fire the blood of ordinary men
And turn preordinance and first decree
Into the law of children. Be not fond,
40   To think that Caesar bears such rebel blood
That will be thawed from the true quality
With that which melteth fools—I mean, sweet words,
Low-crookèd curtsies, and base spaniel fawning.
Thy brother by decree is banishèd.
45   If thou dost bend and pray and fawn for him,
I spurn thee like a cur out of my way.
Know, Caesar doth not wrong, nor without cause
Will he be satisfied.

METELLUS
Is there no voice more worthy than my own
50   To sound more sweetly in great Caesar's ear
For the repealing of my banished brother?

BRUTUS
(kneeling) I kiss thy hand, but not in flattery, Caesar,
Desiring thee that Publius Cimber may
Have an immediate freedom of repeal.

BRUTUS

They're speaking to him. Go up there and second his petition.

CINNA

Casca, you'll be the first to raise your hand.

CAESAR

Are we all ready? What problem should I discuss with you first?

METELLUS

(kneeling) Most high, most mighty, and most powerful Caesar, Metellus Cimber kneels before you with a humble heart—

CAESAR

I have to stop you, Cimber. These kneelings and humble courtesies might excite ordinary men, flattering them into turning Roman law into children's games. But don't be so foolish as to think you can sway *me* from what's right by using the tactics that persuade fools—I mean this flattery, low bows, and puppy-like fawning. Your brother has been banished by decree. If you kneel and beg and flatter for him, I'll kick you out of my way like I would a dog. Know that I am not unjust, and I will not grant him a pardon without reason.

METELLUS

Is there no voice worthier than my own to appeal to Caesar to repeal the order that my brother be banished?

BRUTUS

(kneeling) I kiss your hand, but not in flattery, Caesar. I ask you to repeal Publius Cimber's banishment immediately.

CAESAR
55   What, Brutus?

CASSIUS
     (kneeling)   Pardon, Caesar. Caesar, pardon.
     As low as to thy foot doth Cassius fall
     To beg enfranchisement for Publius Cimber.

CAESAR
     I could be well moved if I were as you.
     If I could pray to move, prayers would move me.
60   But I am constant as the northern star,
     Of whose true-fixed and resting quality
     There is no fellow in the firmament.
     The skies are painted with unnumbered sparks.
     They are all fire and every one doth shine,
65   But there's but one in all doth hold his place.
     So in the world. 'Tis furnished well with men,
     And men are flesh and blood, and apprehensive,
     Yet in the number I do know but one
     That unassailable holds on his rank,
70   Unshaked of motion. And that I am he
     Let me a little show it even in this:
     That I was constant Cimber should be banished,
     And constant do remain to keep him so.

CINNA
     (kneeling) O Caesar—

CAESAR
75   Hence! Wilt thou lift up Olympus?

DECIUS
     (kneeling) Great Caesar—

CAESAR
     Doth not Brutus bootless kneel?

CASCA
     Speak, hands, for me!

CAESAR

What, even you, Brutus?

CASSIUS

(kneeling) Pardon him, Caesar, pardon him. I fall to your feet to beg you to restore Publius Cimber to citizenship.

CAESAR

I could be convinced if I were like you. If I could beg others to change their minds, begging would convince me, too. But I'm as immovable as the northern star, whose stable and stationary quality has no equal in the sky. The sky shows countless stars. They're all made of fire, and each one shines. But only one among all of them remains in a fixed position. So it is on earth. The world is full of men, and men are flesh and blood, and they are capable of reason. Yet out of all of them, I know only one who is unassailable, who never moves from his position. To show you that that's me, let me prove it a little even in this case. I was firm in ordering that Cimber be banished, and I remain firm in that decision.

CINNA

(kneeling) Oh, Caesar—

CAESAR

Enough! Would you try to lift Mount Olympus?

DECIUS

(kneeling) Great Caesar—

CAESAR

Haven't I resisted even Brutus, begging from his knees?

CASCA

Hands, speak for me!

CASCA *and the other conspirators stab* CAESAR, BRUTUS *last*

CAESAR
>*Et tu, Bruté?*—Then fall, Caesar.
>*(dies)*

CINNA
80   Liberty! Freedom! Tyranny is dead!
>Run hence, proclaim, cry it about the streets.

CASSIUS
>Some to the common pulpits, and cry out,
>"Liberty, freedom, and enfranchisement!"

Confusion. Exeunt some plebians and senators

BRUTUS
>People and senators, be not affrighted.
85   Fly not. Stand still. Ambition's debt is paid.

CASCA
>Go to the pulpit, Brutus.

DECIUS
>And Cassius too.

BRUTUS
>Where's Publius?

CINNA
>Here, quite confounded with this mutiny.

METELLUS
90   Stand fast together, lest some friend of Caesar's
>Should chance—

BRUTUS
>Talk not of standing.—Publius, good cheer.
>There is no harm intended to your person,
>Nor to no Roman else. So tell them, Publius.

CASCA and the other conspirators stab CAESAR. BRUTUS stabs him last.

CAESAR

And you too, Brutus? In that case, die, Caesar.
(he dies)

CINNA

Liberty! Freedom! Tyranny is dead! Run and proclaim it in the streets.

CASSIUS

Some should go to the public platforms and cry out, "Liberty, freedom, and democracy!"

Confusion. Some citizens and senators exit.

BRUTUS

People and senators, don't be afraid. Don't run away—stay where you are. Only Caesar had to die for his ambition.

CASCA

Go to the platform, Brutus.

DECIUS

And Cassius too.

BRUTUS

Where's Publius?

CINNA

Here. He's completely stunned by this mutiny.

METELLUS

Stand close together, in case someone loyal to Caesar tries to—

BRUTUS

Don't talk about standing together.—Publius, cheer up. We don't intend any harm to you, nor to anyone else. Tell them this, Publius.

CASSIUS

95   And leave us, Publius, lest that the people,
        Rushing on us, should do your age some mischief.

BRUTUS

        Do so. And let no man abide this deed
        But we the doers.

                                              Exit PUBLIUS

        Enter TREBONIUS

CASSIUS

        Where is Antony?

TREBONIUS

100   Fled to his house amazed.
        Men, wives, and children stare, cry out, and run
        As it were doomsday.

BRUTUS

                            Fates, we will know your pleasures.
        That we shall die, we know. 'Tis but the time,
        And drawing days out, that men stand upon.

                                    finds (+)

CASSIUS

105   Why, he that cuts off twenty years of life
        Cuts off so many years of fearing death.

BRUTUS

        Grant that, and then is death a benefit.
        So are we Caesar's friends, that have abridged
        His time of fearing death. Stoop, Romans, stoop,
110   And let us bathe our hands in Caesar's blood
        Up to the elbows, and besmear our swords.
        Then walk we forth, even to the marketplace,
        And waving our red weapons o'er our heads
        Let's all cry, "Peace, freedom, and liberty!"

CASSIUS

115   Stoop, then, and wash.

CASSIUS

And leave us, Publius, in case the people storming us should harm you.

BRUTUS

Do so. And let no one suffer for this deed except us, the perpetrators.

PUBLIUS exits.

TREBONIUS *enters.*

CASSIUS

Where's Antony?

TREBONIUS

He ran to his house, stunned. Men, wives, and children stare, cry out, and run in the streets as though it were doomsday.

BRUTUS

We'll soon find out what fate has in store for us. All we know is that we'll die sometime, which is all anyone ever knows, though we try to draw out our days for as long as possible.

CASSIUS

Why, the man who shortens his life by twenty years cuts off twenty years of worrying about death.

BRUTUS

So, then, death is a gift, and we are Caesar's friends, for we've done him a service by shortening his time spent fearing death. Kneel, Romans, kneel, and let's wash our hands, up to the elbows, in Caesar's blood and smear it on our swords. Then we'll go out, even to the marketplace, and, waving our bloody swords over our heads, let's cry, "Peace, freedom, and liberty!"

CASSIUS

Kneel then, and wash.

The conspirators smear their hands and swords with
CAESAR's *blood*

                                    How many ages hence
Shall this our lofty scene be acted over
In states unborn and accents yet unknown!

BRUTUS
How many times shall Caesar bleed in sport,
That now on Pompey's basis lies along
120   No worthier than the dust!

CASSIUS
                                    So oft as that shall be,
So often shall the knot of us be called
"The men that gave their country liberty."

DECIUS
What, shall we forth?

CASSIUS
                              Ay, every man away.
Brutus shall lead, and we will grace his heels
125   With the most boldest and best hearts of Rome.

Enter ANTONY'S SERVANT

BRUTUS
Soft! Who comes here? A friend of Antony's.

ANTONY'S SERVANT
(kneeling) Thus, Brutus, did my master bid me kneel.
(falls prostrate) Thus did Mark Antony bid me fall down,
And, being prostrate, thus he bade me say:
130   Brutus is noble, wise, valiant, and honest.
Caesar was mighty, bold, royal, and loving.
Say I love Brutus, and I honor him.
Say I feared Caesar, honored him, and loved him.

The conspirators smear their hands and swords with CAESAR'S *blood.*

How many years from now will this heroic scene be reenacted in countries that don't even exist yet and in languages not yet known!

BRUTUS

How many times will Caesar bleed again in show, though he now lies at the base of Pompey's statue, as worthless as dust!

CASSIUS

As often as it's replayed, our group will be hailed as the men who gave their country liberty.

DECIUS

Well, should we go out?

CASSIUS

Yes, every man forward. Brutus will lead, and we'll follow him with the boldest and best hearts of Rome.

ANTONY'S SERVANT *enters.*

BRUTUS

Wait a minute. Who's that coming? It's a friend of Antony's.

ANTONY'S SERVANT

(kneeling) Brutus, my master ordered me to kneel like this. *(he kneels, head bowed low)* He ordered me to kneel low, and, from the ground, like this, he ordered me to say: "Brutus is noble, wise, brave, and honest. Caesar was mighty, bold, royal, and loving. Antony loves Brutus and honors him. Antony feared Caesar, honored him, and loved him.

If Brutus will vouchsafe that Antony
135   May safely come to him and be resolved
How Caesar hath deserved to lie in death,
Mark Antony shall not love Caesar dead
So well as Brutus living, but will follow
The fortunes and affairs of noble Brutus
140   Thorough the hazards of this untrod state
With all true faith. So says my master Antony.

BRUTUS
Thy master is a wise and valiant Roman.
I never thought him worse.
Tell him, so please him come unto this place,
145   He shall be satisfied and, by my honor,
Depart untouched.

ANTONY'S SERVANT
(rising)   I'll fetch him presently.

Exit **ANTONY'S SERVANT**

BRUTUS
I know that we shall have him well to friend.

CASSIUS
I wish we may. But yet have I a mind
That fears him much, and my misgiving still
150   Falls shrewdly to the purpose.

Enter **ANTONY**

BRUTUS
But here comes Antony.—Welcome, Mark Antony.

ANTONY
O mighty Caesar! Dost thou lie so low?
Are all thy conquests, glories, triumphs, spoils,
Shrunk to this little measure? Fare thee well.
155   —I know not, gentlemen, what you intend,
Who else must be let blood, who else is rank.

If Brutus will swear that Antony may come to him safely and be convinced that Caesar deserved to be killed, Mark Antony will love dead Caesar not nearly as much as living Brutus, and with true faith he'll follow the destiny and affairs of noble Brutus through the difficulties of this unprecedented state of affairs." That's what my master, Antony, says.

BRUTUS

Your master is a wise and honorable Roman. I never thought any less of him. Tell him, if he comes here, I'll explain everything to him and, on my word, he'll leave unharmed.

ANTONY'S SERVANT

(getting up) I'll get him now.

ANTONY'S SERVANT *exits.*

BRUTUS

I know that he'll be on our side.

CASSIUS

I hope we can count on him, but I still fear him, and my hunches are usually accurate.

ANTONY *enters.*

BRUTUS

But here comes Antony.—Welcome, Mark Antony.

ANTONY

Oh, mighty Caesar! Do you lie so low? Have all your conquests, glories, triumphs, achievements, come to so little? Farewell. Gentlemen, I don't know what you intend to do, who else you intend to kill, who else you consider corrupt.

If I myself, there is no hour so fit
As Caesar's death's hour, nor no instrument
Of half that worth as those your swords, made rich
160   With the most noble blood of all this world.
I do beseech ye, if you bear me hard,
Now, whilst your purpled hands do reek and smoke,
Fulfill your pleasure. Live a thousand years,
I shall not find myself so apt to die.
165   No place will please me so, no mean of death,
As here by Caesar, and by you cut off,
The choice and master spirits of this age.

BRUTUS
O Antony, beg not your death of us.
Though now we must appear bloody and cruel—
170   As by our hands and this our present act
You see we do—yet see you but our hands
And this the bleeding business they have done.
Our hearts you see not. They are pitiful.
And pity to the general wrong of Rome—
175   As fire drives out fire, so pity pity—
Hath done this deed on Caesar. For your part,
To you our swords have leaden points, Mark Antony.
Our arms in strength of malice and our hearts
Of brothers' temper do receive you in
180   With all kind love, good thoughts, and reverence.

CASSIUS
Your voice shall be as strong as any man's
In the disposing of new dignities.

BRUTUS
Only be patient till we have appeased
The multitude, beside themselves with fear,
185   And then we will deliver you the cause,
Why I, that did love Caesar when I struck him,
Have thus proceeded.

If it's me, there's no time as good as this hour of Caesar's death, and no weapon better than your swords, covered with the noblest blood in the world. I ask you, if you have a grudge against me, to kill me now, while your stained hands still reek of blood. I could live a thousand years and I wouldn't be as ready to die as I am now. There's no place I'd rather die than here by Caesar, and no manner of death would please me more than being stabbed by you, the masters of this new era.

BRUTUS

Oh, Antony, don't beg us to kill you. Though we seem bloody and cruel right now, with our bloody hands and this deed we've done, you've only seen our hands and their bloody business; you haven't looked into our hearts. They are full of pity for Caesar. But a stronger pity, for the wrongs committed against Rome, drove out our pity for Caesar, as fire drives out fire, and so we killed him. For you, our swords have blunt edges, too dull to harm you, Mark Antony. Our arms, which can be strong and cruel, and our hearts, filled with brotherly love, embrace you with kind love, good thoughts, and reverence.

CASSIUS

Your vote will be as strong as anyone's in the reordering of the government.

BRUTUS

But just be patient until we've calmed the masses, who are beside themselves with fear. Then we'll explain to you why I, who loved Caesar even while I stabbed him, have taken this course of action.

ANTONY

                            I doubt not of your wisdom.
Let each man render me his bloody hand.
(shakes hands with the conspirators)
First, Marcus Brutus, will I shake with you.
190 —Next, Caius Cassius, do I take your hand.
—Now, Decius Brutus, yours.—Now yours, Metellus.
—Yours, Cinna.—And, my valiant Casca, yours.
—Though last, not last in love, yours, good Trebonius.
—Gentlemen all, alas, what shall I say?
195 My credit now stands on such slippery ground
That one of two bad ways you must conceit me,
Either a coward or a flatterer
—That I did love thee, Caesar, O, 'tis true.
If then thy spirit look upon us now,
200 Shall it not grieve thee dearer than thy death
To see thy Antony making his peace,
Shaking the bloody fingers of thy foes—
Most noble!—in the presence of thy corse?
Had I as many eyes as thou hast wounds,
205 Weeping as fast as they stream forth thy blood,
It would become me better than to close
In terms of friendship with thine enemies.
Pardon me, Julius! Here wast thou bayed, brave hart;
Here didst thou fall; and here thy hunters stand,
210 Signed in thy spoil, and crimsoned in thy lethe.
O world, thou wast the forest to this hart,
And this indeed, O world, the heart of thee.
How like a deer, strucken by many princes,
Dost thou here lie!

CASSIUS

215 Mark Antony—

ANTONY

Pardon me, Caius Cassius.
The enemies of Caesar shall say this;
Then, in a friend, it is cold modesty.

ANTONY

I don't doubt your wisdom. Each of you, give me your bloody hand. *(he shakes hands with the conspirators)* First, Marcus Brutus, I shake your hand. Next, Caius Cassius, I take your hand. Now, Decius Brutus, yours. Now yours, Metellus. Yours, Cinna. And yours, my brave Casca. Last but not least, yours, good Trebonius. You are all gentlemen—alas, what can I say? Now that I've shaken your hands, you'll take me for either a coward or a flatterer—in either case, my credibility stands on slippery ground. It's true that I loved you, Caesar—nothing could be truer. If your spirit is looking down upon us now, it must hurt you more than even your death to see your Antony making peace—shaking the bloody hands of your enemies— in front of your corpse. If I had as many eyes as you have wounds, and they wept as fast as your wounds stream blood—even that would be more becoming than joining your enemies in friendship. Forgive me, Julius! On this very spot you were hunted down, like a brave deer. And here you fell, where your hunters are now standing. The spot is marked by your death and stained by your blood. Oh world, you were the forest to this deer, and this deer, oh world, was your dear. Now you lie here, stabbed by many princes!

CASSIUS

Mark Antony—

ANTONY

Pardon me, Caius Cassius. Even Caesar's enemies would say the same. From a friend, it's a cool assessment—no more than that.

CASSIUS
> I blame you not for praising Caesar so.
220 > But what compact mean you to have with us?
> Will you be pricked in number of our friends?
> Or shall we on, and not depend on you?

ANTONY
> Therefore I took your hands, but was indeed
> Swayed from the point by looking down on Caesar.
225 > Friends am I with you all and love you all
> Upon this hope: that you shall give me reasons
> Why and wherein Caesar was dangerous.

BRUTUS
> Or else were this a savage spectacle!
> Our reasons are so full of good regard
230 > That were you, Antony, the son of Caesar,
> You should be satisfied.

ANTONY
>   That's all I seek.
> And am moreover suitor that I may
> Produce his body to the marketplace,
> And in the pulpit, as becomes a friend,
235 > Speak in the order of his funeral.

BRUTUS
> You shall, Mark Antony.

CASSIUS
>   Brutus, a word with you.
> *(aside to* BRUTUS*)* You know not what you do.
> Do not consent
> That Antony speak in his funeral.
240 > Know you how much the people may be moved
> By that which he will utter?

BRUTUS
> *(aside to* CASSIUS*)*   By your pardon.
> I will myself into the pulpit first,
> And show the reason of our Caesar's death.

CASSIUS

I don't blame you for praising Caesar like this, but what agreement do you intend to reach with us? Will you be counted as our friend, or should we proceed without depending on you?

ANTONY

I took your hands in friendship, but, indeed, I was distracted when I looked down at Caesar. I am friends with you all and love you all, on one condition—that you prove to me that Caesar was dangerous.

BRUTUS

Without that proof, this would've been a savage action! Our reasons are so well considered that even if you, Antony, were Caesar's son, you would be satisfied with them.

ANTONY

That's all I ask—and that you let me carry his body to the marketplace and, as a friend ought to do, stand on the platform and give a proper funeral oration.

BRUTUS

You may, Mark Antony.

CASSIUS

Brutus, may I have a word with you? *(speaking so that only* BRUTUS *can hear)* You don't know what you're doing. Don't let Antony speak at his funeral. Don't you know how much the people could be affected by what he says?

BRUTUS

(speaking so that only CASSIUS *can hear)* With your permission, I'll stand on the platform first and explain the reason for Caesar's death.

What Antony shall speak, I will protest,
245   He speaks by leave and by permission,
And that we are contented Caesar shall
Have all true rites and lawful ceremonies.
It shall advantage more than do us wrong.

CASSIUS
(aside to BRUTUS*)* I know not what may fall. I like it not.

BRUTUS
250   Mark Antony, here, take you Caesar's body.
You shall not in your funeral speech blame us,
But speak all good you can devise of Caesar,
And say you do 't by our permission.
Else shall you not have any hand at all
255   About his funeral. And you shall speak
In the same pulpit whereto I am going,
After my speech is ended.

ANTONY
Be it so.
I do desire no more.

BRUTUS
260   Prepare the body then, and follow us.

Exeunt. Manet ANTONY

ANTONY
O, pardon me, thou bleeding piece of earth,
That I am meek and gentle with these butchers!
Thou art the ruins of the noblest man
That ever livèd in the tide of times.
265   Woe to the hand that shed this costly blood!
Over thy wounds now do I prophesy—
Which, like dumb mouths, do ope their ruby lips
To beg the voice and utterance of my tongue—
A curse shall light upon the limbs of men.

What Antony says, I'll announce, he says only by our permission and by our conviction that Caesar should be honored with all the usual and lawful ceremonies. It'll help us more than hurt us.

CASSIUS

(speaking so that only BRUTUS *can hear)* I'm worried about the outcome of his speech. I don't like this plan.

BRUTUS

Mark Antony, take Caesar's body. You will not blame us in your funeral speech, but will say all the good you want to about Caesar and that you do it by our permission. Otherwise, you'll have no role at all in his funeral. And you'll speak on the same platform as I do, after I'm done.

ANTONY

So be it. I don't want anything more.

BRUTUS

Prepare the body, then, and follow us.

Everyone except ANTONY *exits.*

ANTONY

Oh, pardon me, you bleeding corpse, for speaking politely and acting mildly with these butchers! You are what's left of the noblest man that ever lived. Pity the hand that shed this valuable blood. Over your wounds—which, like speechless mouths, open their red lips, as though to beg me to speak—I predict that a curse will fall upon the bodies of men.

270 Domestic fury and fierce civil strife
Shall cumber all the parts of Italy.
Blood and destruction shall be so in use,
And dreadful objects so familiar,
That mothers shall but smile when they behold
275 Their infants quartered with the hands of war,
All pity choked with custom of fell deeds,
And Caesar's spirit, ranging for revenge,
With Ate by his side come hot from hell,
Shall in these confines with a monarch's voice
280 Cry "Havoc!" and let slip the dogs of war,
That this foul deed shall smell above the earth
With carrion men, groaning for burial.

Enter OCTAVIUS' SERVANT

You serve Octavius Caesar, do you not?

OCTAVIUS' SERVANT
I do, Mark Antony.

ANTONY
285 Caesar did write for him to come to Rome.

OCTAVIUS' SERVANT
He did receive his letters and is coming.
And bid me say to you by word of mouth—
(sees CAESAR*'s body)* O Caesar!—

ANTONY
Thy heart is big. Get thee apart and weep.
290 Passion, I see, is catching, for mine eyes,
Seeing those beads of sorrow stand in thine,
Began to water. Is thy master coming?

OCTAVIUS' SERVANT
He lies tonight within seven leagues of Rome.

Fierce civil war will paralyze all of Italy. Blood and destruction will be so common and familiar that mothers will merely smile when their infants are cut to pieces by the hands of war. People's capacity for sympathy will grow tired and weak from the sheer quantity of cruel deeds. And Caesar's ghost, searching for revenge with the goddess Ate by his side, just up from Hell, will cry in the voice of a king, "Havoc!" and unleash the dogs of war. This foul deed will stink up to the sky with men's corpses, which will beg to be buried.

Ate is the Greek goddess of discord and vengeance.

OCTAVIUS'S SERVANT *enters.*

You serve Octavius Caesar, right?

OCTAVIUS'S SERVANT
I do, Mark Antony.

ANTONY
Caesar wrote for him to come to Rome.

OCTAVIUS'S SERVANT
He received Caesar's letters, and he is coming. He told me to say to you—*(seeing* CAESAR'S *body)* Oh, Caesar!—

ANTONY
Your heart is big; go ahead and weep. Grief seems to be contagious, for my eyes, seeing the tears in yours, began to fill. Is your master coming?

OCTAVIUS'S SERVANT
He rests tonight within twenty-one miles of Rome.

ANTONY
>   Post back with speed, and tell him what hath chanced.
> 295   Here is a mourning Rome, a dangerous Rome,
>   No Rome of safety for Octavius yet.
>   Hie hence, and tell him so.—Yet, stay awhile.
>   Thou shalt not back till I have borne this corse
>   Into the marketplace. There shall I try,
> 300   In my oration, how the people take
>   The cruèl issue of these bloody men.
>   According to the which, thou shalt discourse
>   To young Octavius of the state of things.
>   Lend me your hand.

Exeunt with CAESAR'*s body*

ANTONY

Report back to him fast and tell him what has happened. This is now a Rome in mourning, a dangerous Rome. It's not safe enough for Octavius yet. Hurry away and tell him so. No, wait, stay a minute. Don't go back until I've carried the corpse into the marketplace. There I'll use my speech to test what the people think of these bloody men's cruel action. You'll report back to young Octavius how they respond. Help me here.

They exit with CAESAR'*s body.*

ACT 3, SCENE 2

Enter BRUTUS *and* CASSIUS *with the* PLEBEIANS

PLEBEIANS
We will be satisfied! Let us be satisfied!

BRUTUS
Then follow me and give me audience, friends.
—Cassius, go you into the other street
And part the numbers.
5 —Those that will hear me speak, let 'em stay here.
Those that will follow Cassius, go with him,
And public reasons shall be renderèd
Of Caesar's death.

FIRST PLEBEIAN
                                    I will hear Brutus speak.

ANOTHER PLEBEIAN
I will hear Cassius and compare their reasons
10 When severally we hear them renderèd.

                                    Exit CASSIUS *with some of the* PLEBEIANS
                         BRUTUS *goes into the pulpit*

THIRD PLEBEIAN
The noble Brutus is ascended. Silence!

BRUTUS
Be patient till the last.
Romans, countrymen, and lovers! Hear me for my cause,
and be silent that you may hear. Believe me for mine honor,
15 and have respect to mine honor that you may believe.
Censure me in your wisdom, and awake your senses that
you may the better judge. If there be any in this assembly,
any dear friend of Caesar's, to him I say that Brutus' love to
Caesar was no less than his. If then that friend demand why
20 Brutus rose against Caesar, this is my answer: not that I
loved Caesar less, but that I loved Rome more.

ACT 3, SCENE 2

Plebeians = the
common people of
Rome

BRUTUS *and* CASSIUS *enter with a throng of* PLEBEIANS.

PLEBEIANS

> We want answers. Give us answers.

BRUTUS

Then follow me and listen to my speech, friends. Cassius, go to the next street and divide the crowd. Let those who will hear me speak stay. Lead those away who will follow you, and we'll explain publicly the reasons for Caesar's death.

FIRST PLEBEIAN

I'll listen to Brutus.

SECOND PLEBEIAN

I'll listen to Cassius, and we will compare their reasons.

CASSIUS *exits with some of the* PLEBEIANS. BRUTUS *gets up on the platform.*

THIRD PLEBEIAN

Quiet! Noble Brutus has mounted the platform.

BRUTUS

Be patient until I finish. Romans, countrymen, and friends! Listen to my reasons and be silent so you can hear. Believe me on my honor and keep my honor in mind, so you may believe me. Be wise when you criticize me and keep your minds alert so you can judge me fairly. If there's anyone in this assembly, any dear friend of Caesar's, I say to him that my love for Caesar was no less than his. If, then, that friend demands to know why I rose up against Caesar, this is my answer: it's not that I loved Caesar less, but that I loved Rome more.

Had you rather Caesar were living and die all slaves, than
that Caesar were dead, to live all free men? As Caesar loved
me, I weep for him. As he was fortunate, I rejoice at it. As
25 he was valiant, I honor him. But, as he was ambitious, I slew
him. There is tears for his love, joy for his fortune, honor for
his valor, and death for his ambition. Who is here so base
that would be a bondman? If any, speak—for him have I
offended. Who is here so rude that would not be a Roman?
30 If any, speak—for him have I offended. Who is here so vile
that will not love his country? If any, speak—for him have
I offended. I pause for a reply.

ALL

None, Brutus, none.

BRUTUS

Then none have I offended. I have done no more to Caesar
35 than you shall do to Brutus. The question of his death is
enrolled in the Capitol. His glory not extenuated wherein
he was worthy, nor his offenses enforced for which he
suffered death.

Enter Mark **ANTONY** *with* **CAESAR**'s *body*

Here comes his body, mourned by Mark Antony, who,
40 though he had no hand in his death, shall receive the benefit
of his dying—a place in the commonwealth—as which of
you shall not? With this I depart: that, as I slew my best
lover for the good of Rome, I have the same dagger for
myself when it shall please my country to need my death.

ALL

45 Live, Brutus! Live, live!

FIRST PLEBEIAN

Bring him with triumph home unto his house!

Would you rather that Caesar were living and we would all go to our graves as slaves, or that Caesar were dead and we all lived as free men? I weep for Caesar in that he was good to me. I rejoice in his good fortune. I honor him for being brave. But his ambition—for that, I killed him. There are tears for his love, joy for his fortune, honor for his bravery, and death for his ambition. Who here is so low that he wants to be a slave? If there are any, speak, for it is he whom I've offended. Who here is so barbarous that he doesn't want to be a Roman? If there are any, speak, for it is he whom I've offended. Who here is so vile that he doesn't love his country? If there are any, speak, for it is he whom I have offended. I will pause for a reply.

ALL

No one, Brutus, no one.

BRUTUS

Then I have offended no one. I've done no more to Caesar than you will do to me. The reasons for his death are recorded in the Capitol. His glory has not been diminished where he earned it, nor have those offenses for which he was killed been exaggerated.

justifies the kill b/c he's still glorious

ANTONY *enters with* CAESAR'*s body.*

Here comes his body, mourned by Mark Antony, who, though he had no part in the killing, will benefit from his death—receiving a share in the commonwealth, as you all will. With these words I leave. Just as I killed my best friend for the good of Rome, so will I kill myself when my country requires my death.

ALL

Live, Brutus! Live, live!

FIRST PLEBEIAN

Let's carry him in triumph to his house!

SECOND PLEBEIAN
Give him a statue with his ancestors!

THIRD PLEBEIAN
Let him be Caesar!

FOURTH PLEBEIAN
Caesar's better parts
Shall be crowned in Brutus!

FIRST PLEBEIAN
50 We'll bring him to his house with shouts and clamors.

BRUTUS
My countrymen—

SECOND PLEBEIAN
Peace, silence! Brutus speaks.

FIRST PLEBEIAN
Peace, ho!

BRUTUS
Good countrymen, let me depart alone.
And, for my sake, stay here with Antony.
55 Do grace to Caesar's corpse, and grace his speech
Tending to Caesar's glories, which Mark Antony
By our permission is allowed to make.
I do entreat you, not a man depart,
Save I alone, till Antony have spoke.

Exit BRUTUS

FIRST PLEBEIAN
60 Stay, ho! And let us hear Mark Antony.

THIRD PLEBEIAN
Let him go up into the public chair.
We'll hear him.—Noble Antony, go up.

ANTONY
For Brutus' sake, I am beholding to you.
(ascends the pulpit)

SECOND PLEBEIAN

Let's build a statue of him, near those of his ancestors!

THIRD PLEBEIAN

Let him become Caesar!

FOURTH PLEBEIAN

Caesar's better qualities exist in Brutus, and we will crown him.

FIRST PLEBEIAN

We'll bring him to his house with shouts and celebration!

BRUTUS

My countrymen—

SECOND PLEBEIAN

Silence! Brutus speaks.

FIRST PLEBEIAN

Quiet there!

BRUTUS

Good countrymen, let me leave alone. I want you to stay here with Antony to pay respects to Caesar's corpse and listen to Antony's speech about Caesar's glories, which he gives with our permission. I ask that none of you leave, except myself, until Antony has finished.

BRUTUS *exits.*

FIRST PLEBEIAN

Let's stay and hear Mark Antony.

THIRD PLEBEIAN

Let him mount the pulpit. We'll listen to him. Noble Antony, mount the podium.

ANTONY

For Brutus's sake, I am indebted to you.
(he steps up into the pulpit)

FOURTH PLEBEIAN
What does he say of Brutus?

THIRD PLEBEIAN
                                        He says for Brutus' sake
65   He finds himself beholding to us all.

FOURTH PLEBEIAN
'Twere best he speak no harm of Brutus here.

FIRST PLEBEIAN
This Caesar was a tyrant.

THIRD PLEBEIAN
                                        Nay, that's certain.
We are blest that Rome is rid of him.

FOURTH PLEBEIAN
Peace! Let us hear what Antony can say.

ANTONY
70   You gentle Romans—

ALL
                                    Peace, ho! Let us hear him.

ANTONY
Friends, Romans, countrymen, lend me your ears.
I come to bury Caesar, not to praise him.
The evil that men do lives after them;
The good is oft interrèd with their bones.
75   So let it be with Caesar. The noble Brutus
Hath told you Caesar was ambitious.
If it were so, it was a grievous fault,
And grievously hath Caesar answered it.
Here, under leave of Brutus and the rest—
80   For Brutus is an honorable man;
So are they all, all honorable men—
Come I to speak in Caesar's funeral.
He was my friend, faithful and just to me.
But Brutus says he was ambitious,
85   And Brutus is an honorable man.
He hath brought many captives home to Rome
Whose ransoms did the general coffers fill.

FOURTH PLEBEIAN

What does he say about Brutus?

THIRD PLEBEIAN

He says that for Brutus's sake he finds himself indebted to us all.

FOURTH PLEBEIAN

He'd better not speak badly of Brutus here.

FIRST PLEBEIAN

Caesar was a tyrant.

THIRD PLEBEIAN

That's for sure. We're lucky that Rome is rid of him.

SECOND PLEBEIAN

Quiet! Let's hear what Antony has to say.

ANTONY

You gentle Romans—

ALL

Quiet there! Let us hear him.

ANTONY

Friends, Romans, countrymen, give me your attention. I have come here to bury Caesar, not to praise him. The evil that men do is remembered after their deaths, but the good is often buried with them. It might as well be the same with Caesar. The noble Brutus told you that Caesar was ambitious. If that's true, it's a serious fault, and Caesar has paid seriously for it. With the permission of Brutus and the others—for Brutus is an honorable man; they are all honorable men—I have come here to speak at Caesar's funeral. He was my friend, he was faithful and just to me. But Brutus says he was ambitious, and Brutus is an honorable man. He brought many captives home to Rome whose ransoms brought wealth to the city.

Did this in Caesar seem ambitious?
When that the poor have cried, Caesar hath wept.
90   Ambition should be made of sterner stuff.
Yet Brutus says he was ambitious,
And Brutus is an honorable man.
You all did see that on the Lupercal
I thrice presented him a kingly crown,
95   Which he did thrice refuse. Was this ambition?
Yet Brutus says he was ambitious,
And, sure, he is an honorable man.
I speak not to disprove what Brutus spoke,
But here I am to speak what I do know.
100   You all did love him once, not without cause.
What cause withholds you then to mourn for him?
O judgment! Thou art fled to brutish beasts,
And men have lost their reason. Bear with me.
My heart is in the coffin there with Caesar,
105   And I must pause till it come back to me. *(weeps)*

FIRST PLEBEIAN
Methinks there is much reason in his sayings.

SECOND PLEBEIAN
If thou consider rightly of the matter,
Caesar has had great wrong.

THIRD PLEBEIAN
                     Has he, masters?
I fear there will a worse come in his place.

FOURTH PLEBEIAN
110   Marked ye his words? He would not take the crown.
Therefore 'tis certain he was not ambitious.

FIRST PLEBEIAN
If it be found so, some will dear abide it.

SECOND PLEBEIAN
Poor soul! His eyes are red as fire with weeping.

THIRD PLEBEIAN
There's not a nobler man in Rome than Antony.

Is this the work of an ambitious man? When the poor cried, Caesar cried too. Ambition shouldn't be so soft. Yet Brutus says he was ambitious, and Brutus is an honorable man. You all saw that on the Lupercal feast day I offered him a king's crown three times, and he refused it three times. Was this ambition? Yet Brutus says he was ambitious. And, no question, Brutus is an honorable man. I am not here to disprove what Brutus has said, but to say what *I* know. You all loved him once, and not without reason. Then what reason holds you back from mourning him now? Men have become brutish beasts and lost their reason! Bear with me. My heart is in the coffin there with Caesar, and I must pause until it returns to me. *(he weeps)*

FIRST PLEBEIAN
I think there's a lot of sense in what he says.

SECOND PLEBEIAN
If you think about it correctly, Caesar has suffered a great wrong.

THIRD PLEBEIAN
Has he, sirs? I'm worried there will be someone worse to replace him.

FOURTH PLEBEIAN
Did you hear Antony? Caesar wouldn't take the crown. Therefore it's certain that he wasn't ambitious.

FIRST PLEBEIAN
If it turns out he wasn't, certain people are going to get it.

SECOND PLEBEIAN
Poor man! Antony's eyes are fiery red from crying.

THIRD PLEBEIAN
There isn't a nobler man than Antony in all of Rome.

FOURTH PLEBEIAN

115 Now mark him. He begins again to speak.

ANTONY

But yesterday the word of Caesar might
Have stood against the world. Now lies he there,
And none so poor to do him reverence.
O masters, if I were disposed to stir

120 Your hearts and minds to mutiny and rage,
I should do Brutus wrong, and Cassius wrong—
Who, you all know, are honorable men.
I will not do them wrong. I rather choose
To wrong the dead, to wrong myself and you,

125 Than I will wrong such honorable men.
But here's a parchment with the seal of Caesar.
I found it in his closet. 'Tis his will.
Let but the commons hear this testament—
Which, pardon me, I do not mean to read—

130 And they would go and kiss dead Caesar's wounds
And dip their napkins in his sacred blood,
Yea, beg a hair of him for memory,
And, dying, mention it within their wills,
Bequeathing it as a rich legacy

135 Unto their issue.

FOURTH PLEBEIAN

We'll hear the will. Read it, Mark Antony!

ALL

The will, the will! We will hear Caesar's will.

ANTONY

Have patience, gentle friends. I must not read it.
It is not meet you know how Caesar loved you.

140 You are not wood, you are not stones, but men.
And, being men, bearing the will of Caesar,
It will inflame you, it will make you mad.
'Tis good you know not that you are his heirs.
For, if you should—Oh, what would come of it!

FOURTH PLEBEIAN
> Now listen, he's going to speak again.

ANTONY
> Only yesterday the word of Caesar might have stood against the world. Now he lies there worth nothing, and no one is so humble as to show him respect. Oh, sirs, if I stirred your hearts and minds to mutiny and rage, I would offend Brutus and Cassius, who, you all know, are honorable men. I will not do them wrong. I would rather wrong the dead, and wrong myself and you, than wrong such honorable men. But here's a paper with Caesar's seal on it. I found it in his room—it's his will. If you could only hear this testament—which, excuse me, I don't intend to read aloud—you would kiss dead Caesar's wounds and dip your hand-kerchiefs in his sacred blood, and beg for a lock of hair to remember him by. And when you died, you would mention the handkerchief or the hair in your will, bequeathing it to your heirs like a rich legacy.

FOURTH PLEBEIAN
> We want to hear the will. Read it, Mark Antony.

ALL
> The will, the will! We want to hear Caesar's will.

ANTONY
> Be patient, gentle friends, I must not read it. It isn't proper for you to know how much Caesar loved you. You aren't wood, you aren't stones—you're men. And, being men, the contents of Caesar's will would enrage you. It's better that you don't know you're his heirs, for if you knew, just imagine what would come of it!

FOURTH PLEBEIAN
145   Read the will. We'll hear it, Antony.
        You shall read us the will, Caesar's will.

ANTONY
        Will you be patient? Will you stay awhile?
        I have o'ershot myself to tell you of it.
        I fear I wrong the honorable men
150   Whose daggers have stabbed Caesar. I do fear it.

FOURTH PLEBEIAN
        They were traitors! "Honorable men"!

ALL
        The will! The testament!

SECOND PLEBEIAN
        They were villains, murderers. The will! Read the will!

ANTONY
        You will compel me, then, to read the will?
155   Then make a ring about the corpse of Caesar,
        And let me show you him that made the will.
        Shall I descend? And will you give me leave?

ALL
        Come down.

SECOND PLEBEIAN
                        Descend.

THIRD PLEBEIAN
                                        You shall have leave.

        ANTONY *descends from the pulpit*

FOURTH PLEBEIAN
                                                        A ring!
        Stand round.

FIRST PLEBEIAN
                        Stand from the hearse. Stand from the body.

SECOND PLEBEIAN
160   Room for Antony, most noble Antony!

FOURTH PLEBEIAN

Read the will. We want to hear it, Antony. You have to read us the will, Caesar's will.

ANTONY

Will you be patient? Will you wait awhile? I've said too much in telling you of it. I'm afraid that I wrong the honorable men whose daggers have stabbed Caesar.

FOURTH PLEBEIAN

They were traitors. "Honorable men!"

ALL

The will! The testament!

SECOND PLEBEIAN

They were villains, murderers. The will! Read the will!

ANTONY

You force me to read the will, then? Then make a circle around Caesar's corpse, and let me show you the man who made this will. Shall I come down? Will you let me?

ALL

Come down.

SECOND PLEBEIAN

Descend.

THIRD PLEBEIAN

We'll let you.

ANTONY *descends from the pulpit.*

FOURTH PLEBEIAN

Make a circle; stand around him.

FIRST PLEBEIAN

Stand away from the hearse. Stand away from the body.

SECOND PLEBEIAN

Make room for Antony, most noble Antony!

ANTONY
Nay, press not so upon me. Stand far off.

ALL
Stand back. Room! Bear back.

ANTONY
If you have tears, prepare to shed them now.
You all do know this mantle. I remember
165 The first time ever Caesar put it on.
'Twas on a summer's evening in his tent,
That day he overcame the Nervii.
Look, in this place ran Cassius' dagger through.
See what a rent the envious Casca made.
170 Through this the well-belovèd Brutus stabbed.
And as he plucked his cursèd steel away,
Mark how the blood of Caesar followed it,
As rushing out of doors, to be resolved
If Brutus so unkindly knocked, or no.
175 For Brutus, as you know, was Caesar's angel.
Judge, O you gods, how dearly Caesar loved him!
This was the most unkindest cut of all.
For when the noble Caesar saw him stab,
Ingratitude, more strong than traitors' arms,
180 Quite vanquished him. Then burst his mighty heart,
And, in his mantle muffling up his face,
Even at the base of Pompey's statue,
Which all the while ran blood, great Caesar fell.
O, what a fall was there, my countrymen!
185 Then I, and you, and all of us fell down,
Whilst bloody treason flourished over us.
Oh, now you weep, and, I perceive, you feel
The dint of pity. These are gracious drops.
Kind souls, what, weep you when you but behold
190 Our Caesar's vesture wounded? Look you here,
Here is himself, marred, as you see, with traitors.
(lifts up CAESAR'S *mantle)*

ANTONY

No, don't press up against me. Stand further away.

ALL

Stand back. Give him room.

ANTONY

If you have tears, prepare to shed them now. You all know this cloak. I remember the first time Caesar ever put it on. It was a summer's evening; he was in his tent. It was the day he overcame the Nervii warriors. Look, here's where Cassius's dagger pierced it. See the wound that Casca made. Through this hole beloved Brutus stabbed. And when he pulled out his cursed dagger, see how Caesar's blood came with it, as if rushing out a door to see if it was really Brutus who was knocking so rudely. For Brutus, as you know, was Caesar's angel. The gods know how dearly Caesar loved him! This was the most unkind cut of all. For when the noble Caesar saw him stab, he understood his beloved Brutus's ingratitude; it was stronger than the violence of traitors, and it defeated him, bursting his mighty heart. And at the base of Pompey's statue, with his cloak covering his face, which was dripping with blood the whole time, great Caesar fell. Oh, what a fall it was, my countrymen! Then you and I and all of us fell down, while bloody treason triumphed. Oh, now you weep, and I sense that you feel pity. These are gracious tears. But if it overwhelms you to look at Caesar's wounded cloak, how will you feel, kind men, now? Look at this, here is the man—scarred, as you can see, by traitors. *(he lifts up* CAESAR's *cloak)*

FIRST PLEBEIAN
O piteous spectacle!

SECOND PLEBEIAN
                    O noble Caesar!

THIRD PLEBEIAN
O woeful day!

FOURTH PLEBEIAN
O traitors, villains!

FIRST PLEBEIAN
                    O most bloody sight!

SECOND PLEBEIAN
195   We will be revenged.

ALL
        Revenge! About! Seek! Burn! Fire! Kill! Slay!
        Let not a traitor live!

ANTONY
                    Stay, countrymen.

FIRST PLEBEIAN
Peace there! Hear the noble Antony.

SECOND PLEBEIAN
We'll hear him. We'll follow him. We'll die with him.

ANTONY
200   Good friends, sweet friends! Let me not stir you up
        To such a sudden flood of mutiny.
        They that have done this deed are honorable.
        What private griefs they have, alas, I know not,
        That made them do it. They are wise and honorable,
205   And will, no doubt, with reasons answer you.
        I come not, friends, to steal away your hearts.
        I am no orator, as Brutus is,
        But, as you know me all, a plain blunt man
        That love my friend. And that they know full well
210   That gave me public leave to speak of him.
        For I have neither wit nor words nor worth,
        Action nor utterance nor the power of speech,

FIRST PLEBEIAN
Oh, what a sad sight!

SECOND PLEBEIAN
Oh, noble Caesar!

THIRD PLEBEIAN
Oh, sad day!

FOURTH PLEBEIAN
Oh, traitors, villains!

FIRST PLEBEIAN
Oh, most bloody sight!

SECOND PLEBEIAN
We will get revenge.

ALL
Revenge! Let's go after them! Seek! Burn! Set fire! Kill! Slay! Leave no traitors alive!

ANTONY
Wait, countrymen.

FIRST PLEBEIAN
Quiet there! Listen to the noble Antony.

SECOND PLEBEIAN
We'll listen to him, we'll follow him, we'll die with him.

ANTONY
Good friends, sweet friends, don't let me stir you up to such a sudden mutiny. Those who have done this deed are honorable. I don't know what private grudges they had that made them do it. They're wise and honorable, and will no doubt give you reasons for it. I haven't come to steal your loyalty, friends. I'm no orator, as Brutus is. I'm only, as you know, a plain, blunt man who loved his friend, and the men who let me speak know this well. I have neither cleverness nor rhetorical skill nor the authority nor gesture nor eloquence nor the power of speech to stir men up. I just speak directly. I tell you what you already know. I show you sweet Caesar's wounds—poor, speechless

To stir men's blood. I only speak right on.
I tell you that which you yourselves do know,
215 Show you sweet Caesar's wounds, poor poor dumb mouths,
And bid them speak for me. But were I Brutus,
And Brutus Antony, there were an Antony
Would ruffle up your spirits and put a tongue
In every wound of Caesar that should move
220 The stones of Rome to rise and mutiny.

ALL
We'll mutiny.

FIRST PLEBEIAN
            We'll burn the house of Brutus.

THIRD PLEBEIAN
Away, then! Come, seek the conspirators.

ANTONY
Yet hear me, countrymen. Yet hear me speak.

ALL
Peace, ho! Hear Antony. Most noble Antony!

ANTONY
225 Why, friends, you go to do you know not what.
Wherein hath Caesar thus deserved your loves?
Alas, you know not. I must tell you then.
You have forgot the will I told you of.

ALL
Most true. The will! Let's stay and hear the will.

ANTONY
230 Here is the will, and under Caesar's seal
To every Roman citizen he gives—
To every several man—seventy-five drachmas.

SECOND PLEBEIAN
Most noble Caesar! We'll revenge his death.

THIRD PLEBEIAN
O royal Caesar!

ANTONY
            Hear me with patience.

mouths!—and make them speak for me. But if I were Brutus and Brutus were me, then I'd stir you up, and install in each of Caesar's wounds the kind of voice that could convince even stones to rise up and mutiny.

ALL

We'll mutiny.

FIRST PLEBEIAN

We'll burn Brutus's house.

THIRD PLEBEIAN

Let's go, then! Come, find the conspirators!

ANTONY

Wait, and listen to me, countrymen.

ALL

Quiet! Wait! Listen to Antony. Most noble Antony!

ANTONY

Why, friends, you don't even know what you're doing yet. What has Caesar done to deserve your love? Alas, you don't know. I must tell you then. You've forgotten the will I told you about.

ALL

Yes! The will! Let's stay and hear the will!

ANTONY

Here's the will, written under Caesar's seal. To every Roman citizen he gives—to every individual man—seventy-five drachmas.

SECOND PLEBEIAN

Most noble Caesar! We'll revenge his death.

THIRD PLEBEIAN

Oh, royal Caesar!

ANTONY

Listen to me patiently.

ALL

Peace, ho!

ANTONY

235   Moreover, he hath left you all his walks,
His private arbors and new-planted orchards,
On this side Tiber. He hath left them you
And to your heirs forever—common pleasures,
To walk abroad and recreate yourselves.
240   Here was a Caesar! When comes such another?

FIRST PLEBEIAN

Never, never.—Come, away, away!
We'll burn his body in the holy place,
And with the brands fire the traitors' houses.
Take up the body.

SECOND PLEBEIAN

Go fetch fire.

THIRD PLEBEIAN

245   Pluck down benches.

FOURTH PLEBEIAN

Pluck down forms, windows, anything.

Exeut PLEBEIANS *with* CAESAR's *body*

ANTONY

Now let it work. Mischief, thou art afoot.
Take thou what course thou wilt!

Enter OCTAVIUS' SERVANT

How now, fellow?

OCTAVIUS' SERVANT

Sir, Octavius is already come to Rome.

ANTONY

250   Where is he?

OCTAVIUS' SERVANT

He and Lepidus are at Caesar's house.

ALL

> Quiet, there!

ANTONY

> Also, he's left you all his walkways—in his private gardens and newly planted orchards—on this side of the Tiber River. He's left them to you and to your heirs forever—public pleasures in which you will be able to stroll and relax. Here was a Caesar! When will there be another like him?

FIRST PLEBEIAN

> Never, never. Let's go! We'll burn his body in the holy place and use the brands to set the traitors' houses on fire. Take up the body.

SECOND PLEBEIAN

> We'll start a fire.

THIRD PLEBEIAN

> We'll use benches for wood—

FOURTH PLEBEIAN

> And windowsills, anything.

Citizens exit with CAESAR'*s body.*

ANTONY

> Now, let it work. Trouble, you have begun—take whatever course you choose!

OCTAVIUS'S SERVANT *enters.*

> What's up, my man?

OCTAVIUS'S SERVANT

> Sir, Octavius has already arrived in Rome.

ANTONY

> Where is he?

OCTAVIUS'S SERVANT

> He and Lepidus are at Caesar's house.

ANTONY

And thither will I straight to visit him.
He comes upon a wish. Fortune is merry,
And in this mood will give us anything.

OCTAVIUS' SERVANT

255   I heard him say, Brutus and Cassius
Are rid like madmen through the gates of Rome.

ANTONY

Belike they had some notice of the people
How I had moved them. Bring me to Octavius.

Exeunt

ANTONY

I will go straight to visit him. I ask for him, and he comes. Fortune is happy today and, in this mood, will give us anything we want.

OCTAVIUS'S SERVANT

I heard Octavius say that Brutus and Cassius have ridden like madmen through the gates of Rome.

ANTONY

They probably received warning about how much I stirred up the people. Take me to Octavius.

They exit.

ACT 3, SCENE 3

Enter CINNA THE POET, *and after him the* PLEBEIANS

CINNA THE POET
I dreamt tonight that I did feast with Caesar,
And things unlucky charge my fantasy.
I have no will to wander forth of doors,
Yet something leads me forth.

FIRST PLEBEIAN
5   What is your name?

SECOND PLEBEIAN
Whither are you going?

THIRD PLEBEIAN
Where do you dwell?

FOURTH PLEBEIAN
Are you a married man or a bachelor?

SECOND PLEBEIAN
Answer every man directly.

FIRST PLEBEIAN
10   Ay, and briefly.

FOURTH PLEBEIAN
Ay, and wisely.

THIRD PLEBEIAN
Ay, and truly, you were best.

CINNA THE POET
What is my name? Whither am I going? Where do I dwell?
Am I a married man or a bachelor? Then, to answer every
15   man directly and briefly, wisely and truly—wisely I say, I
am a bachelor.

SECOND PLEBEIAN
That's as much as to say they are fools that marry. You'll
bear me a bang for that, I fear. Proceed, directly.

CINNA THE POET
Directly, I am going to Caesar's funeral.

ACT 3, SCENE 3

CINNA THE POET *enters, followed by* PLEBEIANS.

CINNA THE POET
> I dreamed last night that I feasted with Caesar, and unlucky signs overwhelmed my imagination. I have no desire to go outside, yet something leads me there.

FIRST PLEBEIAN
> What's your name?

SECOND PLEBEIAN
> Where are you going?

THIRD PLEBEIAN
> Where do you live?

FOURTH PLEBEIAN
> Are you a married man or a bachelor?

SECOND PLEBEIAN
> Answer all of us, now.

FIRST PLEBEIAN
> Yes, and be brief.

FOURTH PLEBEIAN
> Yes, and be wise.

THIRD PLEBEIAN
> Yes, and be truthful, if you know what's good for you.

CINNA THE POET
> What's my name? Where am I going? Where do I live? Am I a married man or a bachelor? Then, to answer every man briefly, wisely, and truthfully—wisely I say, I am a bachelor.

SECOND PLEBEIAN
> You imply that married men are fools. You'll get a blow from me for that, I think. Go on with what you were saying—right this instant.

CINNA THE POET
> Right this instant, I'm going to Caesar's funeral.

FIRST PLEBEIAN
20   As a friend or an enemy?

CINNA THE POET
        As a friend.

SECOND PLEBEIAN
        That matter is answered directly.

FOURTH PLEBEIAN
        For your dwelling—briefly.

CINNA THE POET
        Briefly, I dwell by the Capitol.

THIRD PLEBEIAN
25   Your name, sir, truly.

CINNA THE POET
        Truly, my name is Cinna.

FIRST PLEBEIAN
        Tear him to pieces. He's a conspirator.

CINNA THE POET
        I am Cinna the poet. I am Cinna the poet.

FOURTH PLEBEIAN
        Tear him for his bad verses! Tear him for his bad verses!

CINNA THE POET
30   I am not Cinna the conspirator.

FOURTH PLEBEIAN
        It is no matter. His name's Cinna. Pluck but his name out
        of his heart and turn him going.

THIRD PLEBEIAN
        Tear him, tear him!

PLEBEIANS *attack* **CINNA THE POET**

ALL
        Come, brands, ho, firebrands. To Brutus', to Cassius',
35   burn all. Some to Decius' house and some to Casca's. Some
        to Ligarius'. Away, go!

Exeunt **PLEBEIANS** *dragging* **CINNA THE POET**

FIRST PLEBEIAN
> As a friend or an enemy?

CINNA THE POET
> As a friend.

SECOND PLEBEIAN
> He answered that question straight.

FOURTH PLEBEIAN
> As for where you live, tell us quickly—get to the point.

CINNA THE POET
> Getting right to the point, I live near the Capitol.

THIRD PLEBEIAN
> Tell us your name, sir, truthfully.

CINNA THE POET
> Truthfully, my name is Cinna.

FIRST PLEBEIAN
> Tear him to pieces. He's a conspirator.

CINNA THE POET
> I am Cinna the poet, I am Cinna the poet!

FOURTH PLEBEIAN
> Tear him apart for his bad verses, tear him up!

CINNA THE POET
> I'm not Cinna the conspirator.

FOURTH PLEBEIAN
> It doesn't matter. His name's Cinna. Pull only his name out of his heart and let him go.

bye honor?

THIRD PLEBEIAN
> Tear him apart, tear him up!

The PLEBEIANS *attack* CINNA THE POET.

ALL
> Come, firebrands, over here! To Brutus's, to Cassius's, let's burn them all. Some of you go to Decius's house and some to Casca's. Some to Ligarius's. Go!

The PLEBEIANS *exit, dragging* CINNA THE POET.

ACT FOUR
SCENE 1

Enter ANTONY, OCTAVIUS, *and* LEPIDUS

ANTONY
These many, then, shall die. Their names are pricked.

OCTAVIUS
(to LEPIDUS*)*
Your brother too must die. Consent you, Lepidus?

LEPIDUS
I do consent—

OCTAVIUS
               Prick him down, Antony.

LEPIDUS
Upon condition Publius shall not live,
5 Who is your sister's son, Mark Antony.

ANTONY
He shall not live. Look, with a spot I damn him.
But, Lepidus, go you to Caesar's house.
Fetch the will hither, and we shall determine
How to cut off some charge in legacies.

LEPIDUS
10 What, shall I find you here?

OCTAVIUS
Or here, or at the Capitol.

Exit LEPIDUS

ANTONY
This is a slight, unmeritable man,
Meet to be sent on errands. Is it fit,
The threefold world divided, he should stand
15 One of the three to share it?

ACT FOUR
SCENE 1

ANTONY, OCTAVIUS, *and* LEPIDUS *enter.*

ANTONY

These ones, then, will be assassinated. Their names are marked.

OCTAVIUS

(to LEPIDUS*)* Your brother has to die too. Do you agree, Lepidus?

LEPIDUS

I agree—

OCTAVIUS

Put a mark next to his name too, Antony.

LEPIDUS

On the condition that your sister's son, Publius, also must die, Mark Antony.

ANTONY

He will die. See—I've sealed his fate with this mark next to his name. But, Lepidus, go to Caesar's house. Bring his will here, and we'll figure out a way to reduce his bequests to the people.

LEPIDUS

Will you be here when I return?

OCTAVIUS

Either here or at the Capitol.

LEPIDUS *exits.*

ANTONY

He's an unremarkable man, fit only to be sent on errands. Does it really make sense, once we divide the world into three parts, that he should be one of the three rulers?

OCTAVIUS
                                        So you thought him.
And took his voice who should be pricked to die
In our black sentence and proscription.

ANTONY
Octavius, I have seen more days than you.
And though we lay these honors on this man
20   To ease ourselves of divers slanderous loads,
He shall but bear them as the ass bears gold,
To groan and sweat under the business,
Either led or driven, as we point the way.
And having brought our treasure where we will,
25   Then take we down his load and turn him off,
Like to the empty ass, to shake his ears
And graze in commons.

OCTAVIUS
                                    You may do your will,
But he's a tried and valiant soldier.

ANTONY
So is my horse, Octavius, and for that
30   I do appoint him store of provender.
It is a creature that I teach to fight,
To wind, to stop, to run directly on,
His corporal motion governed by my spirit,
And, in some taste, is Lepidus but so.
35   He must be taught and trained and bid go forth,
A barren-spirited fellow, one that feeds
On objects, arts, and imitations,
Which, out of use and staled by other men,
Begin his fashion. Do not talk of him
40   But as a property. And now, Octavius,
Listen great things. Brutus and Cassius
Are levying powers. We must straight make head.
Therefore let our alliance be combined,
Our best friends made, our means stretched.

OCTAVIUS

You thought it made sense, and you listened to him about who should be marked to die in these harsh death sentences.

ANTONY

Octavius, I'm older than you are. And although we're giving these honors to this man so that he shares some of the blame for what we're doing, he'll carry these honors like a jackass carries gold—groaning and sweating under the load, either led or pushed, as we direct him. Once he's carried our treasure where we want it, we'll free him of the load and turn him loose like a jackass, to shake his ears and graze in the public pastures.

OCTAVIUS

You can do what you want, but he's an experienced and honorable soldier.

ANTONY

So is my horse, Octavius, and for that reason I give him all the hay he wants. But my horse is a creature that *I* teach to fight—to turn, to stop, to run in a straight line. I govern the motion of his body. And in some ways, Lepidus is just like that. He has to be taught and trained and told to go forward. He's an empty man, who pays attention to fashions and tastes that other men took up and got tired of long ago. Don't think about Lepidus except as a means to an end. And now, Octavius, listen to more important things. Brutus and Cassius are raising armies. We have to raise our own immediately. So, we should combine forces and organize our allies, pull together our friends, and stretch our resources as far as they'll go.

45   And let us presently go sit in council
        How covert matters may be best disclosed,
        And open perils surest answered.

OCTAVIUS
        Let us do so. For we are at the stake
        And bayed about with many enemies.
50   And some that smile have in their hearts, I fear,
        Millions of mischiefs.

                                                    Exeunt

Let's immediately organize a council to discuss the best way to find out their secrets and the safest way to confront the threats we're already faced with.

OCTAVIUS

Let's do that, because we're hemmed in by many enemies. And even some of the people who smile at us are in fact plotting against us, I'm afraid.

They exit.

ACT 4, SCENE 2

Drum. Enter BRUTUS *with* LUCIUS, LUCILLIUS, *and the army.*
TITINIUS *and* PINDARUS *meet them*

BRUTUS
Stand, ho!

LUCILLIUS
Give the word, ho, and stand.

BRUTUS
What now, Lucillius? Is Cassius near?

LUCILLIUS
He is at hand, and Pindarus is come
5   To do you salutation from his master.

BRUTUS
He greets me well.—Your master, Pindarus,
In his own change or by ill officers
Hath given me some worthy cause to wish
Things done, undone. But if he be at hand
10   I shall be satisfied.

PINDARUS
                              I do not doubt
But that my noble master will appear
Such as he is, full of regard and honor.

BRUTUS
He is not doubted.—A word, Lucillius.
(takes LUCILLIUS *aside)*
How he received you, let me be resolved.

LUCILLIUS
15   With courtesy and with respect enough.
But not with such familiar instances
Nor with such free and friendly conference
As he hath used of old.

BRUTUS
                              Thou hast described
A hot friend cooling. Ever note, Lucillius,

ACT 4, SCENE 2

A drum plays. BRUTUS, LUCILLIUS, LUCIUS, *and* SOL-
DIERS *enter.* TITINIUS *and* PINDARUS *meet them.*

BRUTUS

Stop.

LUCILLIUS

Pass on the command to halt!

BRUTUS

What's happening now, Lucillius? Is Cassius nearby?

LUCILLIUS

He's nearby, and Pindarus has come to salute you on
behalf of his master.

BRUTUS

He sends his greetings through a good man. Your master, Pindarus, either because he's changed his mind or
been influenced by bad officers, has made me wish we
hadn't done some of the things we did. If he's nearby,
I want an explanation.

PINDARUS

I have no doubt that my noble master will prove himself to be what he is: honorable and noble.

BRUTUS

I don't doubt him. Can I have a word with you, Lucillius? *(takes* LUCILLIUS *aside)* Tell me how Cassius
treated you. Put my mind at rest.

LUCILLIUS

He received me with courtesy and sufficient respect,
but not with affection, nor with as much open and
friendly conversation as he once greeted me.

BRUTUS

You've described a warm friend who's cooling off.
Remember this, Lucillius. When a friend starts to get

20 When love begins to sicken and decay,
    It useth an enforcèd ceremony.
    There are no tricks in plain and simple faith.
    But hollow men, like horses hot at hand,
    Make gallant show and promise of their mettle.

    Low march within

25 But when they should endure the bloody spur,
    They fall their crests and, like deceitful jades,
    Sink in the trial. Comes his army on?

LUCILLIUS
    They mean this night in Sardis to be quartered.
    The greater part, the horse in general,
30 Are come with Cassius.

BRUTUS
                            Hark! He is arrived.
    March gently on to meet him.

    Enter CASSIUS *and his powers*

CASSIUS
    Stand, ho!

BRUTUS
    Stand, ho! Speak the word along.

FIRST SOLDIER
    Stand!

SECOND SOLDIER
35 Stand!

THIRD SOLDIER
    Stand!

CASSIUS
    Most noble brother, you have done me wrong.

BRUTUS
    Judge me, you gods! Wrong I mine enemies?
    And if not so, how should I wrong a brother?

sick of you, he treats you artificially. Plain and simple loyalty doesn't make anyone act phony. But insincere men, like horses who are too lively at the start of a race, make a big show of their spirit.

A low sound of drums and SOLDIERS *marching.*

But when push comes to shove, they droop like those horses that are all show and slow to a crawl. Is his army approaching?

LUCILLIUS

They plan to spend the night in Sardis. The larger part, the main body of cavalry, are coming with Cassius.

BRUTUS

Look! He's arrived. March to meet him at a dignified pace.

CASSIUS *enters with his army.*

CASSIUS

Halt.

BRUTUS

Halt! Pass the order along.

FIRST SOLDIER

Halt!

SECOND SOLDIER

Halt!

THIRD SOLDIER

Halt!

CASSIUS

Most noble brother, you have done me wrong.

BRUTUS

Let the gods judge me! Do I mistreat even my enemies? No. So how could I possibly wrong a brother?

CASSIUS
40   Brutus, this sober form of yours hides wrongs.
        And when you do them—

BRUTUS
                                Cassius, be content.
        Speak your griefs softly. I do know you well.
        Before the eyes of both our armies here,
        Which should perceive nothing but love from us,
45   Let us not wrangle. Bid them move away.
        Then in my tent, Cassius, enlarge your griefs,
        And I will give you audience.

CASSIUS
                                Pindarus,
        Bid our commanders lead their charges off
        A little from this ground.

BRUTUS
50   Lucillius, do you the like. And let no man
        Come to our tent till we have done our conference.
        Let Lucius and Titinius guard our door.

                                                        Exeunt

CASSIUS

> Brutus, your sober expression is a mask to hide the fact that you've wronged me. And when you do—

BRUTUS

> Cassius, calm down. We know each other well, and you can speak your grievances quietly. Let's not argue here in front of both our armies, which ought to see nothing but love between us. Order them to move back. Then, in my tent, you can elaborate on your complaints, and I'll listen.

CASSIUS

> Pindarus, order our commanders to lead their charges a little ways away from this ground.

BRUTUS

> Lucillius, you do the same, and don't allow anyone to come into our tent until we've finished our conference. Have Lucius and Titinius guard the door.

> *Everyone except* BRUTUS *and* CASSIUS *exits.*

ACT 4, SCENE 3

Manent BRUTUS *and* CASSIUS, *now in the tent*

CASSIUS
> That you have wronged me doth appear in this:
> You have condemned and noted Lucius Pella
> For taking bribes here of the Sardians,
> Wherein my letters, praying on his side
5> Because I knew the man, were slighted off.

BRUTUS
> You wronged yourself to write in such a case.

CASSIUS
> In such a time as this it is not meet
> That every nice offense should bear his comment.

BRUTUS
> Let me tell you, Cassius, you yourself
10> Are much condemned to have an itching palm,
> To sell and mart your offices for gold
> To undeservers.

CASSIUS
>   I "an itching palm"!
> You know that you are Brutus that speak this,
> Or, by the gods, this speech were else your last.

BRUTUS
15> The name of Cassius honors this corruption,
> And chastisement doth therefore hide his head.

CASSIUS
> Chastisement!

BRUTUS
> Remember March, the ides of March remember.
> Did not great Julius bleed for justice' sake?

ACT 4, SCENE 3

BRUTUS *and* CASSIUS *remain onstage. They are now in their tent.*

CASSIUS

My evidence that you have wronged me is that you condemned and disgraced Lucius Pella for taking bribes here from the Sardinians, and you ignored my letters, where I argued that he was innocent; I know the man.

BRUTUS

You wronged yourself to write on behalf of such a man.

CASSIUS

In a time like this, it doesn't make sense to criticize every offense.

BRUTUS

I'll tell you, Cassius, you yourself have been called greedy and been accused of giving your positions to undeserving men in exchange for gold.

CASSIUS

Me, "greedy"! You know, if you were anyone other than Brutus, that speech would be your last.

BRUTUS

The name of Cassius gives credit to these corrupt actions, and so they go unpunished.

CASSIUS

Unpunished!

BRUTUS

Remember March, March 15th. Didn't great Caesar bleed for the sake of justice?

20   What villain touched his body, that did stab,
      And not for justice? What, shall one of us
      That struck the foremost man of all this world
      But for supporting robbers, shall we now
      Contaminate our fingers with base bribes,
25   And sell the mighty space of our large honors
      For so much trash as may be graspèd thus?
      I had rather be a dog and bay the moon
      Than such a Roman.

CASSIUS
                            Brutus, bait not me.
      I'll not endure it. You forget yourself
30   To hedge me in. I am a soldier, I,
      Older in practice, abler than yourself
      To make conditions.

BRUTUS
      Go to. You are not, Cassius.

CASSIUS
      I am.

BRUTUS
35   I say you are not.

CASSIUS
      Urge me no more, I shall forget myself.
      Have mind upon your health, tempt me no further.

BRUTUS
      Away, slight man!

CASSIUS
      Is 't possible?

BRUTUS
40   Hear me, for I will speak.
      Must I give way and room to your rash choler?
      Shall I be frighted when a madman stares?

CASSIUS
      O ye gods, ye gods, must I endure all this?

Who among us stabbed him for any cause but justice? What—did one of us strike down the most powerful man in the world in order to support robbers? Should we now dirty our fingers with lowly bribes and sell the mighty offices that we hold for whatever money we can get our hands on? I'd rather be a dog and howl at the moon than be that kind of Roman.

CASSIUS

Brutus, do not provoke me. I will not take it. You're forgetting yourself when you back me into a corner. I'm a soldier, more experienced than you, and better able to give orders.

BRUTUS

Get lost! You are not, Cassius.

CASSIUS

I am.

BRUTUS

I say you're not.

CASSIUS

Don't provoke me any further or I'll forget to restrain myself. If you care about your health, you won't push me any further.

BRUTUS

Leave, you little man.

CASSIUS

Is this possible?

BRUTUS

Listen to me, for I have something to tell you. Am I required to indulge your rash anger? Does a madman scare me when he stares at me?

CASSIUS

Oh gods, oh gods! Must I endure all this?

BRUTUS
"All this"? Ay, more. Fret till your proud heart break.
45   Go show your slaves how choleric you are
And make your bondmen tremble. Must I budge?
Must I observe you? Must I stand and crouch
Under your testy humor? By the gods,
You shall digest the venom of your spleen,
50   Though it do split you. For from this day forth,
I'll use you for my mirth, yea, for my laughter,
When you are waspish.

CASSIUS
                                    Is it come to this?

BRUTUS
You say you are a better soldier.
Let it appear so. Make your vaunting true,
55   And it shall please me well. For mine own part,
I shall be glad to learn of noble men.

CASSIUS
You wrong me every way. You wrong me, Brutus.
I said an elder soldier, not a better.
Did I say "better"?

BRUTUS
60   If you did, I care not.

CASSIUS
When Caesar lived, he durst not thus have moved me.

BRUTUS
Peace, peace! You durst not so have tempted him.

CASSIUS
I durst not!

BRUTUS
No.

CASSIUS
65   What, durst not tempt him?

BRUTUS

"All this"? Yes, and more. Go ahead—rage till your proud heart breaks. Show your slaves how mad you are, and make your servants tremble. But me—am I going to cower at you and your irritable moods? You'll have to swallow your own poison till it makes you burst before I'm going to respond; from now on, I'll make you the butt of my jokes whenever you get sharp with me.

CASSIUS

Has it come to this?

BRUTUS

You say you're a better soldier. Show it! Make your boasts come true, and I'll be thrilled. I'm always happy to hear about brave men.

CASSIUS

You wrong me in every way. You wrong me, Brutus. I said an *older* soldier, not a better one. Did I say "better"?

BRUTUS

If you did, I don't care.

CASSIUS

When Caesar was alive, even he wouldn't dare anger me like this.

BRUTUS

Oh, be quiet. You wouldn't have dared to tempt him so.

CASSIUS

I wouldn't have dared!

BRUTUS

No.

CASSIUS

What? Not dared to tempt him?

BRUTUS
For your life you durst not.

CASSIUS
Do not presume too much upon my love.
I may do that I shall be sorry for.

BRUTUS
You have done that you should be sorry for.
70   There is no terror, Cassius, in your threats,
For I am armed so strong in honesty
That they pass by me as the idle wind,
Which I respect not. I did send to you
For certain sums of gold, which you denied me,
75   For I can raise no money by vile means.
By heaven, I had rather coin my heart
And drop my blood for drachmas than to wring
From the hard hands of peasants their vile trash
By any indirection. I did send
80   To you for gold to pay my legions,
Which you denied me. Was that done like Cassius?
Should I have answered Caius Cassius so?
When Marcus Brutus grows so covetous
To lock such rascal counters from his friends,
85   Be ready, gods, with all your thunderbolts.
Dash him to pieces!

CASSIUS
                              I denied you not.

BRUTUS
You did.

CASSIUS
                    I did not. He was but a fool that brought
My answer back. Brutus hath rived my heart.
A friend should bear his friend's infirmities,
90   But Brutus makes mine greater than they are.

BRUTUS
I do not, till you practice them on me.

BRUTUS

You wouldn't have dared, out of fear for your life.

CASSIUS

Don't take my love for granted. I might do something I'll be sorry for.

BRUTUS

You've already done something you should be sorry for. Your threats don't scare me, Cassius, because I'm so secure in my honesty and integrity that they pass me by like a weak breeze. I asked you for a certain amount of gold, which you wouldn't give me. I myself can't raise money by unethical means. I'd rather turn my heart into money and my drops of blood into coins than use crooked tactics to wring petty cash from the hardworking hands of peasants. I asked you for gold to pay my soldiers, and you wouldn't give it to me. Was that the Caius Cassius that I knew? And would I have ever done that to you? If I ever get so greedy that I hoard such petty cash from my friends, may the gods dash me to pieces with their thunderbolts!

CASSIUS

I didn't refuse you.

BRUTUS

You did.

CASSIUS

I didn't. The man who brought my answer to you was a fool. You have broken my heart. A friend should put up with his friend's weaknesses, but you exaggerate mine.

BRUTUS

I don't until you practice them on me.

CASSIUS
You love me not.

BRUTUS
                                        I do not like your faults.

CASSIUS
A friendly eye could never see such faults.

BRUTUS
A flatterer's would not, though they do appear
95   As huge as high Olympus.

CASSIUS
Come, Antony, and young Octavius, come,
Revenge yourselves alone on Cassius,
For Cassius is aweary of the world—
Hated by one he loves; braved by his brother;
100   Checked like a bondman, all his faults observed,
Set in a notebook, learned, and conned by rote
To cast into my teeth. Oh, I could weep
My spirit from mine eyes.
(offers BRUTUS *his bared dagger)* There is my dagger.
105   And here my naked breast. Within, a heart
Dearer than Plutus' mine, richer than gold.
If that thou beest a Roman, take it forth.
I, that denied thee gold, will give my heart.
Strike, as thou didst at Caesar. For I know
110   When thou didst hate him worst, thou lovedst him better
Than ever thou lovedst Cassius.

BRUTUS
                                        Sheathe your dagger.
Be angry when you will, it shall have scope.
Do what you will, dishonor shall be humor.
O Cassius, you are yokèd with a lamb
115   That carries anger as the flint bears fire,
Who, much enforcèd, shows a hasty spark
And straight is cold again.

CASSIUS

You don't love me.

BRUTUS

I don't like your faults.

CASSIUS

A friend would never see those faults.

BRUTUS

No, a flatterer wouldn't, even if the faults were as huge as Mount Olympus.

CASSIUS

Come, Antony and young Octavius! Get your revenge on Cassius, because Cassius has grown tired of the world. He's hated by someone he loves, defied by his brother, rebuked like a servant, all his faults observed, catalogued in a notebook, read, and committed to memory so they can be thrown in his face. Oh, I could weep my soul right out of myself! There's my dagger *(he offers* BRUTUS *his unsheathed dagger)*, and here's my bare chest. Inside it is a heart more valuable than Pluto's silver mine and richer than gold. If you're a Roman, take my heart out. I, who denied you gold, will give you my heart. Strike as you did at Caesar, for I know even when you hated him the most, you still loved him better than you ever loved me.

Pluto is the god of the underworld, and Plutus is the god of wealth. The two are often confused or combined, as they are here.

BRUTUS

Put away your dagger. Be angry whenever you like, it's all right with me. Do whatever you want, and I'll say your insults are just a bad mood. Oh, Cassius, you're partners with a quiet lamb. My anger is like a flint striking—a brief spark, and then I'm cold again.

CASSIUS
                              Hath Cassius lived
          To be but mirth and laughter to his Brutus,
          When grief and blood ill-tempered vexeth him?

BRUTUS
120   When I spoke that, I was ill-tempered too.

CASSIUS
          Do you confess so much? Give me your hand.

BRUTUS
          And my heart too.

          CASSIUS *and* BRUTUS *shake hands*

CASSIUS
                              O Brutus!

BRUTUS
                                        What's the matter?

CASSIUS
          Have not you love enough to bear with me,
          When that rash humor which my mother gave me
125   Makes me forgetful?

BRUTUS
                              Yes, Cassius. And from henceforth
          When you are over-earnest with your Brutus,
          He'll think your mother chides and leave you so.

POET
          (within) Let me go in to see the generals.
          There is some grudge between 'em. 'Tis not meet
130   They be alone.

LUCILLIUS
          (within)   You shall not come to them.

POET
          (within) Nothing but death shall stay me.

          Enter a POET *followed by* LUCILLIUS *and* TITINIUS

CASSIUS

Have I lived this long only to be the butt of a joke whenever you're angry or frustrated?

BRUTUS

When I said that, I was angry too.

CASSIUS

You admit it, then? Give me your hand.

BRUTUS

And my heart too.

CASSIUS and BRUTUS shake hands.

CASSIUS

Oh, Brutus!

BRUTUS

What's the matter?

CASSIUS

Do you have enough love for me to be patient when my bad temper, which I inherited from my mother, makes me forget how I should behave?

BRUTUS

Yes, Cassius. And from now on, when you get hot with me, I'll assume it's your mother speaking and leave it at that.

POET

(offstage) Let me in to see the generals. There's a grudge between them, and it isn't a good idea for them to be alone.

LUCILLIUS

(offstage) You can't see them.

POET

(offstage) You'd have to kill me to stop me.

A POET enters, followed by LUCILLIUS and TITINIUS.

CASSIUS
How now? What's the matter?

POET
For shame, you generals! What do you mean?
Love, and be friends as two such men should be.
135 For I have seen more years, I'm sure, than ye.

CASSIUS
Ha, ha, how vilely doth this cynic rhyme!

BRUTUS
(to POET) Get you hence, sirrah. Saucy fellow, hence!

CASSIUS
Bear with him, Brutus. 'Tis his fashion.

BRUTUS
I'll know his humor when he knows his time.
140 What should the wars do with these jigging fools?
—Companion, hence!

CASSIUS
                    Away, away, be gone.

                                        Exit POET

BRUTUS
Lucillius and Titinius, bid the commanders
Prepare to lodge their companies tonight.

CASSIUS
And come yourselves, and bring Messala with you,
145 Immediately to us.

                    Exeunt LUCILLIUS and TITINIUS

BRUTUS
(calls off)   Lucius, a bowl of wine!

CASSIUS
I did not think you could have been so angry.

CASSIUS

What's this! What's the matter?

POET

You should be ashamed, generals! What do you think you're doing?
Love each other and be friends, like two such men should be.
Listen to me, because I'm older than you, surely.

CASSIUS

Ha ha! This man's rhymes are terrible!

BRUTUS

(to POET) Get out of here, you! Get away, you rude fellow!

CASSIUS

Be patient with him, Brutus. That's just how he is.

BRUTUS

I'll humor him when he learns how to behave. What should we do with all these rhyming fools that follow us from post to post? Get out of here, my friend.

CASSIUS

Away, away, be gone.

The POET exits.

BRUTUS

Lucillius and Titinius, order the commanders to have the men camp for the night.

CASSIUS

And return to us immediately, bringing Messala with you.

LUCILLIUS and TITINIUS exit.

BRUTUS

(calling offstage) Lucius, bring a bowl of wine.

CASSIUS

I didn't think you could even be so angry.

BRUTUS
O Cassius, I am sick of many griefs.

CASSIUS
Of your philosophy you make no use
If you give place to accidental evils.

BRUTUS
150 No man bears sorrow better. Portia is dead.

CASSIUS
Ha, Portia?

BRUTUS
She is dead.

CASSIUS
How 'scaped I killing when I crossed you so?
O insupportable and touching loss!
155 Upon what sickness?

BRUTUS
Impatient of my absence,
And grief that young Octavius with Mark Antony
Have made themselves so strong—for with her death
That tidings came—with this she fell distract
And, her attendants absent, swallowed fire.

CASSIUS
160 And died so?

BRUTUS
Even so.

CASSIUS
O ye immortal gods!

Enter LUCIUS *with wine and tapers*

BRUTUS

Oh Cassius, I'm tired out by many sorrows.

CASSIUS

You're forgetting your Stoic philosophy if you allow chance misfortunes to upset you.

The Stoics were philosophers who maintained that people should accept suffering without complaining.

BRUTUS

No one bears sorrow better than me. Portia is dead.

CASSIUS

Portia!

BRUTUS

She is dead.

CASSIUS

How did you manage not to kill me when we argued just now? What an irreplaceable and grievous loss! What sickness did she die of?

BRUTUS

She was worried about my absence, and about the fact that young Octavius and Mark Antony have grown so strong—which I found out at the same time as the news of her death. She became full of despair and, when her attendants were away, swallowed burning coals.

CASSIUS

And that's how she died?

BRUTUS

Yes, like that.

CASSIUS

Oh, immortal gods!

LUCIUS *enters with wine and candles.*

BRUTUS
Speak no more of her.—Give me a bowl of wine.—
In this I bury all unkindness, Cassius.
(drinks)

CASSIUS
My heart is thirsty for that noble pledge.
Fill, Lucius, till the wine o'erswell the cup.
165   I cannot drink too much of Brutus' love.
(drinks)

Exit LUCIUS

Enter TITINIUS *and* MESSALA

BRUTUS
Come in, Titinius.—Welcome, good Messala!
Now sit we close about this taper here
And call in question our necessities.

CASSIUS
Portia, art thou gone?

BRUTUS
No more, I pray you.
170   —Messala, I have here receivèd letters
That young Octavius and Mark Antony
Come down upon us with a mighty power,
Bending their expedition toward Philippi.

MESSALA
Myself have letters of the selfsame tenor.

BRUTUS
175   With what addition?

MESSALA
That by proscription and bills of outlawry,
Octavius, Antony, and Lepidus
Have put to death an hundred senators.

BRUTUS

Don't talk about her anymore. Give me a bowl of wine. With this toast I bury all bad feelings between us, Cassius. *(he drinks)*

CASSIUS

My heart is thirsty for that noble promise. Fill my cup, Lucius, until the wine overflows it. I cannot drink too much of Brutus's love. *(he drinks)*

LUCIUS *exits.*
TITINIUS *and* MESSALA *enter.*

BRUTUS

Come in, Titinius! Welcome, good Messala. Now let's sit closely around this candle and discuss our needs.

CASSIUS

Portia, are you really gone?

BRUTUS

No more about that, please. Messala, I have received these letters explaining that young Octavius and Mark Antony are rushing toward Philippi and bearing down upon us with a mighty power.

MESSALA

I have received letters that say the same.

BRUTUS

And anything else?

MESSALA

That with a series of legal writs, Octavius, Antony, and Lepidus have put a hundred senators to death.

BRUTUS
Therein our letters do not well agree.
180 Mine speak of seventy senators that died
By their proscriptions, Cicero being one.

CASSIUS
Cicero one?

MESSALA
Cicero is dead,
And by that order of proscription.
(to BRUTUS) Had you your letters from your wife, my lord?

BRUTUS
185 No, Messala.

MESSALA
Nor nothing in your letters writ of her?

BRUTUS
Nothing, Messala.

MESSALA
That methinks is strange.

BRUTUS
Why ask you? Hear you aught of her in yours?

MESSALA
No, my lord.

BRUTUS
190 Now, as you are a Roman, tell me true.

MESSALA
Then like a Roman bear the truth I tell.
For certain she is dead, and by strange manner.

BRUTUS
Why, farewell, Portia. We must die, Messala.
With meditating that she must die once,
195 I have the patience to endure it now.

MESSALA
Even so great men great losses should endure.

BRUTUS

On that point, our letters don't agree. My letters say only seventy senators were killed, one being Cicero.

CASSIUS

Cicero too?

MESSALA

Cicero is dead, by their decree. *(to* BRUTUS*)* Have you received letters from your wife, my lord?

BRUTUS

No, Messala.

MESSALA

And you haven't heard any news about her in your letters?

BRUTUS

Nothing, Messala.

MESSALA

I think that's strange.

BRUTUS

Why do you ask? Have you heard something of her in your letters?

MESSALA

No, my lord.

BRUTUS

Now, as you're a Roman, tell me the truth.

MESSALA

Then you must take the truth I have to tell like a Roman. It's certain that she is dead, and she died in a strange way.

BRUTUS

Well, good-bye, Portia. We all must die, Messala. Having already thought about the fact that she would have to die sometime, I can endure her death now.

MESSALA

That's the way great men ought to endure great losses.

CASSIUS
> I have as much of this in art as you,
> But yet my nature could not bear it so.

BRUTUS
> Well, to our work alive. What do you think
> 200   Of marching to Philippi presently?

CASSIUS
> I do not think it good.

BRUTUS
>   Your reason?

CASSIUS
>   This it is:
> 'Tis better that the enemy seek us.
> So shall he waste his means, weary his soldiers,
> Doing himself offense, whilst we, lying still,
> 205   Are full of rest, defense, and nimbleness.

BRUTUS
> Good reasons must of force give place to better.
> The people 'twixt Philippi and this ground
> Do stand but in a forced affection,
> For they have grudged us contribution.
> 210   The enemy, marching along by them,
> By them shall make a fuller number up,
> Come on refreshed, new-added, and encouraged,
> From which advantage shall we cut him off
> If at Philippi we do face him there,
> 215   These people at our back.

CASSIUS
>   Hear me, good brother—

BRUTUS
> Under your pardon. You must note beside,
> That we have tried the utmost of our friends,
> Our legions are brim-full, our cause is ripe.
> The enemy increaseth every day.
> 220   We, at the height, are ready to decline.
> There is a tide in the affairs of men,

CASSIUS

I've practiced Stoicism with as much devotion as you, but I still couldn't bear this news like you do.

BRUTUS

Well, let's move on to our work with the living. What do you think of marching to Philippi immediately?

CASSIUS

I don't think it's a good idea.

BRUTUS

Why not?

CASSIUS

Here's why: it'd be better for the enemy to come after us. That way, he'll waste his provisions and tire out his soldiers, weakening his own capacities, while we, lying still, are rested, energetic, and nimble.

BRUTUS

Your reasons are good, but I have better reasons for doing the opposite. The people who live between here and Philippi are loyal to us only because we force them to be. We made them contribute to our efforts against their will. The enemy, marching past them, will add them to its numbers, then come at us refreshed, newly reinforced, and full of courage. Thus we must cut him off from this advantage. If we meet him at Philippi, these people will be at our backs.

CASSIUS

Listen to me, good brother.

BRUTUS

Begging your pardon, I'll continue what I was saying. You must also take into account that we've gotten as much from our friends as they can give. Our regiments are full to the brim; our cause is ready. The enemy gets larger each day. We, now at our largest, can only decrease. There's a tidal movement in

Which, taken at the flood, leads on to fortune;
Omitted, all the voyage of their life
Is bound in shallows and in miseries.
225 On such a full sea are we now afloat,
And we must take the current when it serves
Or lose our ventures.

CASSIUS

                Then, with your will, go on.
We'll along ourselves, and meet them at Philippi.

BRUTUS

The deep of night is crept upon our talk,
230 And nature must obey necessity,
Which we will niggard with a little rest.
There is no more to say?

CASSIUS

                No more. Good night.
Early tomorrow will we rise and hence.

BRUTUS

Lucius!

Enter LUCIUS

My gown.

                        Exit LUCIUS

           Farewell, good Messala.—
235 Good night, Titinius.—Noble, noble Cassius,
Good night and good repose.

CASSIUS

                O my dear brother,
This was an ill beginning of the night.
Never come such division 'tween our souls.
Let it not, Brutus.

Enter LUCIUS *with the gown*

men's affairs. Seizing the highest tide leads on to fortune. If high tide is let to pass, all the rest of the voyage
of their lives will be marked by difficulty and misery.
It's on such a high tide that we're now floating, and we
must take the current when it is offered, or lose our
campaign.

CASSIUS

If that's what you want, all right. We'll go forward
with you and meet them at Philippi.

BRUTUS

It's now late at night, and actions must accommodate
bodily needs, which we'll satisfy with only a short
rest. That's all there is to say.

CASSIUS

There's nothing else. Good night. We'll rise and leave
early tomorrow.

BRUTUS

Lucius!

LUCIUS *enters.*

My nightgown.

LUCIUS *exits.*

Farewell, good Messala. Good night, Titinius. Noble,
noble Cassius, good night and sleep well.

CASSIUS

Oh my dear brother! This was a bad start to the night.
Let's pray that we never come into conflict like that
again. Let's not, Brutus.

LUCIUS *enters with the nightgown.*

BRUTUS
                        Everything is well.

CASSIUS
240   Good night, my lord.

BRUTUS
                        Good night, good brother.

TITINIUS, MESSALA
          Good night, Lord Brutus.

BRUTUS
          Farewell, everyone.

Exeunt CASSIUS, TITINIUS, *and* MESSALA

          Give me the gown. Where is thy instrument?

LUCIUS
          Here in the tent.

BRUTUS
                        What, thou speak'st drowsily?
245   Poor knave, I blame thee not. Thou art o'erwatched.
          Call Claudio and some other of my men.
          I'll have them sleep on cushions in my tent.

LUCIUS
          Varrus and Claudio!

Enter VARRUS *and* CLAUDIO

VARRUS
                        Calls my lord?

BRUTUS
          I pray you, sirs, lie in my tent and sleep.
250   It may be I shall raise you by and by
          On business to my brother Cassius.

VARRUS
          So please you, we will stand and watch your pleasure.

BRUTUS

Everything's fine.

CASSIUS

Good night, my lord.

BRUTUS

Good night, good brother.

TITINIUS, MESSALA

Good night, Lord Brutus.

BRUTUS

Farewell, everyone.

CASSIUS, TITINIUS, and MESSALA exit.

Give me the gown. Where's your lute?

LUCIUS

Here in the tent.

BRUTUS

What, are you sleepy? Poor boy, I don't blame you; you've stayed awake too long. Call Claudio and some of my other men. I'll have them sleep on cushions in my tent.

LUCIUS

Varrus and Claudio!

VARRUS and CLAUDIO enter.

VARRUS

Did you call, my lord?

BRUTUS

Sirs, I ask you to sleep in my tent. I might wake you up in a while to send you on an errand to my brother Cassius.

VARRUS

If you like, we'll stand by and wait to do whatever you need.

BRUTUS
I will not have it so. Lie down, good sirs.
It may be I shall otherwise bethink me.
255 —Look, Lucius, here's the book I sought for so.
I put it in the pocket of my gown.

VARRUS *and* CLAUDIO *lie down*

LUCIUS
I was sure your lordship did not give it me.

BRUTUS
Bear with me, good boy, I am much forgetful.
Canst thou hold up thy heavy eyes awhile,
260 And touch thy instrument a strain or two?

LUCIUS
Ay, my lord, an 't please you.

BRUTUS
                                                    It does, my boy.
I trouble thee too much, but thou art willing.

LUCIUS
It is my duty, sir.

BRUTUS
I should not urge thy duty past thy might.
265 I know young bloods look for a time of rest.

LUCIUS
I have slept, my lord, already.

BRUTUS
It was well done, and thou shalt sleep again.
I will not hold thee long. If I do live,
I will be good to thee.

LUCIUS *plays music and sings a song, falling asleep*

270 This is a sleepy tune. O murderous slumber,
Layst thou thy leaden mace upon my boy
That plays thee music?—Gentle knave, good night.

BRUTUS

No, please, lie down, good sirs, because I might change my mind. Look, Lucius, here's the book I was searching for. I put it in the pocket of my nightgown.

VARRUS *and* CLAUDIO *lie down.*

LUCIUS

I was sure that you hadn't given it to me.

BRUTUS

Bear with me, good boy. I've become very forgetful. Can you stay awake a bit longer and play a few tunes on your lute?

LUCIUS

Yes, my lord, if you would like.

BRUTUS

I would, my boy. I ask too much of you, but you're always willing.

LUCIUS

It's my duty, sir.

BRUTUS

I shouldn't make you do more than you're able. I know that young men look forward to their rest.

LUCIUS

I've already slept, my lord.

BRUTUS

That was good planning, and you'll sleep some more. I won't keep you very long. If I live through this, I'll be good to you.

LUCIUS *plays music and sings a song, then falls asleep.*

This is a sleepy tune. Oh, deadening sleep, have you taken over my boy who plays music for you? Gentle boy, good night. I won't trouble you so much as to wake you. If you were to droop down, you'd break

I will not do thee so much wrong to wake thee.
If thou dost nod, thou break'st thy instrument.
275   I'll take it from thee. And, good boy, good night.
—Let me see, let me see. Is not the leaf turned down
Where I left reading? Here it is, I think.

Enter the GHOST *of Caesar*

How ill this taper burns!—Ha, who comes here?
I think it is the weakness of mine eyes
280   That shapes this monstrous apparition.
It comes upon me.—Art thou any thing?
Art thou some god, some angel, or some devil
That makest my blood cold and my hair to stare?
Speak to me what thou art.

GHOST
285   Thy evil spirit, Brutus.

BRUTUS
Why comest thou?

GHOST
To tell thee thou shalt see me at Philippi.

BRUTUS
Well, then I shall see thee again?

GHOST
                                        Ay, at Philippi.

BRUTUS
Why, I will see thee at Philippi, then.

Exit GHOST

290   Now I have taken heart thou vanishest.
Ill spirit, I would hold more talk with thee.
—Boy, Lucius!—Varrus!—Claudio!—Sirs, awake!
—Claudio!

LUCIUS
The strings, my lord, are false.

your instrument, and so I'll take it from you. Good
night, good boy. Let me see, let me see. Didn't I turn
down the page where I left off reading? Here it is, I
think. This candle doesn't give much light.

The GHOST *of Caesar enters.*

What! Who goes there? I think it's my bad eyesight
that's making me see this horrible vision. It's coming
toward me. Are you real? Are you a god, an angel, or
a devil, that you make my blood turn cold and my hair
stand up? Tell me what you are.

GHOST

I'm your evil spirit, Brutus.

BRUTUS

Why do you come here?

GHOST

To tell you that you'll see me at Philippi.

BRUTUS

Then I'll see you again?

GHOST

Yes, at Philippi.

BRUTUS

Alright, then I'll see you at Philippi.

The GHOST *exits.*

Just as you go, I find the courage to talk to you. Evil
spirit, I want to talk some more. Boy, Lucius! Varrus!
Claudio! Sirs, awake! Claudio!

LUCIUS

My lord, the strings are out of tune.

BRUTUS
295   He thinks he still is at his instrument.
        Lucius, awake.

LUCIUS
        My lord?

BRUTUS
        Didst thou dream, Lucius, that thou so criedst out?

LUCIUS
        My lord, I do not know that I did cry.

BRUTUS
300   Yes, that thou didst. Didst thou see any thing?

LUCIUS
        Nothing, my lord.

BRUTUS
        Sleep again, Lucius.—Sirrah Claudio!
        (to VARRUS)   Fellow thou, awake!

VARRUS
        My lord?

CLAUDIO
        My lord?

BRUTUS
305   Why did you so cry out, sirs, in your sleep?

VARRUS, CLAUDIO
        Did we, my lord?

BRUTUS
                        Ay. Saw you anything?

VARRUS
        No, my lord, I saw nothing.

CLAUDIO
                        Nor I, my lord.

BRUTUS

He thinks he's still playing his instrument. Lucius, wake up!

LUCIUS

My lord?

BRUTUS

Were you dreaming, Lucius? Is that why you cried out?

LUCIUS

My lord, I don't think I cried out.

BRUTUS

Yes, you did. Did you see anything?

LUCIUS

Nothing, my lord.

BRUTUS

Go back to sleep, Lucius. Claudio! *(to* VARRUS*)* You there, wake up!

VARRUS

My lord?

CLAUDIO

My lord?

BRUTUS

Why did you cry out in your sleep?

VARRUS, CLAUDIO

Did we, my lord?

BRUTUS

Yes. Did you see anything?

VARRUS

No, my lord, I didn't see anything.

CLAUDIO

Me neither, my lord.

BRUTUS
    Go and commend me to my brother Cassius.
    Bid him set on his powers betimes before,
310 And we will follow.

VARRUS, CLAUDIO
                    It shall be done, my lord.

                                    Exeunt severally

BRUTUS

Go to my brother Cassius. Order him to advance his forces first thing, and we'll follow.

VARRUS, CLAUDIO

Yes, my lord.

Everyone exits in different directions.

ACT FIVE
SCENE 1

Enter OCTAVIUS, ANTONY, *and their army*

OCTAVIUS

Now, Antony, our hopes are answerèd.
You said the enemy would not come down
But keep the hills and upper regions.
It proves not so. Their battles are at hand.
They mean to warn us at Philippi here,
Answering before we do demand of them.

ANTONY

Tut, I am in their bosoms, and I know
Wherefore they do it. They could be content
To visit other places, and come down
With fearful bravery, thinking by this face
To fasten in our thoughts that they have courage.
But 'tis not so.

Enter a MESSENGER

MESSENGER

Prepare you, generals.
The enemy comes on in gallant show.
Their bloody sign of battle is hung out,
And something to be done immediately.

ANTONY

Octavius, lead your battle softly on,
Upon the left hand of the even field.

OCTAVIUS

Upon the right hand I. Keep thou the left.

ANTONY

Why do you cross me in this exigent?

ACT FIVE
SCENE 1

OCTAVIUS *and* ANTONY *enter with their army.*

OCTAVIUS

Now, Antony, our prayers have been answered. You said the enemy wouldn't come down but keep to the hills and upper regions. It seems not. Their forces are nearby. They intend to challenge us here at Philippi, responding to our challenge before we've even challenged him.

ANTONY

I know how they think, and I understand why they're doing this. They really wish they were somewhere else, but they want to descend on us, looking fierce so we'll think they're brave. But they aren't.

A MESSENGER *enters.*

MESSENGER

Prepare yourselves, generals. The enemy approaches with great display. They show their bloody heralds of battle, and something must be done immediately.

ANTONY

Octavius, lead your forces slowly out to the left side of the level field.

OCTAVIUS

I'll go to the right side. You stay on the left.

ANTONY

Why are you defying me in this urgent matter?

OCTAVIUS
20   I do not cross you. But I will do so.

March. Drum.
Enter BRUTUS, CASSIUS, *and their army, including* LUCILLIUS,
TITINIUS, *and* MESSALA

BRUTUS
They stand and would have parley.

CASSIUS
Stand fast, Titinius. We must out and talk.

OCTAVIUS
Mark Antony, shall we give sign of battle?

ANTONY
No, Caesar, we will answer on their charge.
25   Make forth. The generals would have some words.

OCTAVIUS
(to his army) Stir not until the signal.

BRUTUS
Words before blows. Is it so, countrymen?

OCTAVIUS
Not that we love words better, as you do.

BRUTUS
Good words are better than bad strokes, Octavius.

ANTONY
30   In your bad strokes, Brutus, you give good words.
Witness the hole you made in Caesar's heart,
Crying "Long live, hail, Caesar!"

CASSIUS
                                    Antony,
The posture of your blows are yet unknown.
But for your words, they rob the Hybla bees
35   And leave them honeyless.

OCTAVIUS

I'm not defying you, but it's what I'm going to do.

The sound of soldiers marching, and a drum. BRUTUS *and* CASSIUS *enter with their army, which includes* LUCILLIUS, TITINIUS, *and* MESSALA.

BRUTUS

They've stopped. They want to talk.

CASSIUS

Stay here, Titinius. We have to go out and talk to them.

OCTAVIUS

Mark Antony, should we give the signal to attack?

ANTONY

No, Octavius Caesar, we'll respond to their charge. Go forward. The generals want to speak with us.

OCTAVIUS

(to his army) Don't move until we give the signal.

BRUTUS

Words before fighting. Is that how it is, countrymen?

OCTAVIUS

Not that we love words more than fighting, like you do.

BRUTUS

Good words are better than bad strokes, Octavius.

ANTONY

Brutus, you give a nice speech along with your evil strokes. Think of the hole you made in Caesar's heart when you cried, "Long live Caesar! Hail Caesar!"

CASSIUS

Antony, we don't yet know what kind of blows you can inflict. But your words are as sweet as honey—you've stolen from the bees and left them with nothing.

ANTONY
> Not stingless too?

BRUTUS
> Oh, yes, and soundless too.
> For you have stol'n their buzzing, Antony,
> And very wisely threat before you sting.

ANTONY
40
> Villains, you did not so when your vile daggers
> Hacked one another in the sides of Caesar.
> You showed your teeth like apes, and fawned like hounds,
> And bowed like bondmen, kissing Caesar's feet,
> Whilst damnèd Casca, like a cur, behind
45
> Struck Caesar on the neck. O you flatterers!

CASSIUS
> Flatterers?—Now, Brutus, thank yourself.
> This tongue had not offended so today
> If Cassius might have ruled.

OCTAVIUS
> Come, come, the cause. If arguing make us sweat,
50
> The proof of it will turn to redder drops.
> *(draws his sword)* Look, I draw a sword against conspirators.
> When think you that the sword goes up again?
> Never, till Caesar's three and thirty wounds
> Be well avenged, or till another Caesar
55
> Have added slaughter to the sword of traitors.

BRUTUS
> Caesar, thou canst not die by traitors' hands
> Unless thou bring'st them with thee.

OCTAVIUS
>   So I hope.
> I was not born to die on Brutus' sword.

BRUTUS
> O, if thou wert the noblest of thy strain,
60
> Young man, thou couldst not die more honorable.

ANTONY

I took their strings too, wouldn't you say?

BRUTUS

Oh, yes, and you've left them silent too, because you stole their buzzing, Antony. You very wisely warn us before you sting.

ANTONY

Villains, you didn't do even that much when your vile daggers struck each other as they hacked up Caesar's sides. You smiled like apes and fawned like dogs and bowed like servants, kissing Caesar's feet. And all the while, damned Casca, like a dog, struck Caesar on the neck from behind. Oh, you flatterers!

CASSIUS

Flatterers! Now, Brutus, you have only yourself to thank. Antony wouldn't be here to offend us today if you'd listened to me earlier.

OCTAVIUS

Come, come, let's remember why we're here. If arguing makes us sweat, the real trial will turn that water to blood. *(he draws his sword)* Look: I draw my sword against conspirators. When do you think I'll put it away? Never, until Caesar's thirty-three wounds are well avenged, or until I too have been killed by you.

BRUTUS

Caesar, you're not going to be killed by a traitor—unless you kill yourself..

OCTAVIUS

I hope you're right. I wasn't born to die on your sword.

BRUTUS

If you were the noblest of your family, young man, you couldn't die more honorably.

CASSIUS
A peevish schoolboy, worthless of such honor,
Joined with a masker and a reveler!

ANTONY
Old Cassius still.

OCTAVIUS
                    Come, Antony, away.—
Defiance, traitors, hurl we in your teeth.
65   If you dare fight today, come to the field.
If not, when you have stomachs.

                    Exeunt OCTAVIUS, ANTONY, *and their army*

CASSIUS
Why, now, blow wind, swell billow, and swim bark!
The storm is up and all is on the hazard.

BRUTUS
Ho, Lucillius, hark, a word with you.

LUCILLIUS
(stands forth)   My lord?

            BRUTUS *and* LUCILLIUS *converse apart*

CASSIUS
70   Messala!

MESSALA
(stands forth)
                    What says my general?

CASSIUS
                                Messala,
This is my birthday, as this very day
Was Cassius born. Give me thy hand, Messala.
Be thou my witness that against my will,
As Pompey was, am I compelled to set
75   Upon one battle all our liberties.

CASSIUS

An annoying schoolboy, unworthy of such an honor, joined by a masquerader and a partier!

ANTONY

Still the same old Cassius!

OCTAVIUS

Come Antony, let's go. Traitors, we defy you. If you dare to fight today, come to the field. If not, come when you have the courage.

OCTAVIUS, ANTONY, and their army exit.

CASSIUS

Now let the wind blow, waves swell, and ships sink! The storm has begun and everything is at stake.

BRUTUS

Lucillius! I'd like a word with you.

LUCILLIUS

(coming forward) My lord?

BRUTUS and LUCILLIUS converse to the side.

CASSIUS

Messala!

MESSALA

(coming forward) What is it, my general?

CASSIUS

Messala, today is my birthday—I was born on this very day. Give me your hand, Messala. You'll be my witness that I've been forced, as Pompey was, to wager all of our freedoms on one battle.

You know that I held Epicurus strong
And his opinion. Now I change my mind,
And partly credit things that do presage.
Coming from Sardis, on our former ensign
80 Two mighty eagles fell, and there they perched,
Gorging and feeding from our soldiers' hands,
Who to Philippi here consorted us.
This morning are they fled away and gone,
And in their steads do ravens, crows, and kites
85 Fly o'er our heads and downward look on us
As we were sickly prey. Their shadows seem
A canopy most fatal, under which
Our army lies, ready to give up the ghost.

MESSALA
Believe not so.

CASSIUS
                    I but believe it partly,
90 For I am fresh of spirit and resolved
To meet all perils very constantly.

BRUTUS
(returning with LUCILLIUS*)* Even so, Lucillius.

CASSIUS
                    Now, most noble Brutus,
The gods today stand friendly that we may,
Lovers in peace, lead on our days to age.
95 But since the affairs of men rest still incertain,
Let's reason with the worst that may befall.
If we do lose this battle, then is this
The very last time we shall speak together.
What are you then determinèd to do?

You know that I used to believe in Epicurus and his disregard for omens. I've changed my mind now and partly believe in omens. Traveling from Sardis, two mighty eagles fell on our front flag and perched there, eating from the hands of the soldiers who'd accompanied us to Philippi. This morning, they've flown away and in their place are ravens, crows, and kites, flying over our heads and looking down on us, as though we were sickly prey. Their shadows are like a deadly canopy, under which our army lies, ready to die.

MESSALA

Don't believe in this.

CASSIUS

I only partly believe it, for I'm enthusiastic and resolved to meet all dangers without wavering.

BRUTUS

(returning with LUCILLIUS*)* —Right, Lucillius.

CASSIUS

Now, most noble Brutus, the gods are friendly with us today so that we, who want peace, can live on to old age! But since the affairs of men are always uncertain, let's think about the worst that may happen. If we lose this battle, this is the last time we'll speak to each other. If we lose, what do you plan to do?

BRUTUS

100 Even by the rule of that philosophy
By which I did blame Cato for the death
Which he did give himself (I know not how,
But I do find it cowardly and vile,
For fear of what might fall, so to prevent
105 The time of life), arming myself with patience
To stay the providence of some high powers
That govern us below.

CASSIUS

Then if we lose this battle
You are contented to be led in triumph
Thorough the streets of Rome?

BRUTUS

110 No, Cassius, no. Think not, thou noble Roman,
That ever Brutus will go bound to Rome.
He bears too great a mind. But this same day
Must end that work the ides of March begun.
And whether we shall meet again I know not.
115 Therefore our everlasting farewell take.
Forever and forever farewell, Cassius.
If we do meet again, why, we shall smile.
If not, why then this parting was well made.

CASSIUS

Forever and forever farewell, Brutus.
120 If we do meet again, we'll smile indeed.
If not, 'tis true this parting was well made.

BRUTUS

Why then, lead on. Oh, that a man might know
The end of this day's business ere it come!
But it sufficeth that the day will end,
125 And then the end is known.—Come, ho! Away!

Exeunt

BRUTUS

By the same principle that made me condemn Cato for committing suicide, I plan to be patient and submit to what the gods decide. I don't know why, but I find it cowardly and vile to kill oneself early to prevent possible suffering later on.

CASSIUS

Then if we lose this battle, you'll be willing to be led in chains through the streets of Rome?

BRUTUS

No, Cassius, no. Don't imagine that I'll ever allow myself to return to Rome in chains. My mind is too great for that. But today, the work that March 15th began must end, and I don't know if we'll meet again. Therefore, accept my everlasting farewell. Forever and forever, farewell, Cassius! If we meet again, then we'll smile. If not, then this parting was well done.

CASSIUS

Forever and forever, farewell, Brutus! If we meet again, then we'll smile indeed. If not, it's true, this parting was well done.

BRUTUS

Well, lead on. Oh, I wish I could know what will happen today before it happens! But it's enough to know that the day will end, and then the end will be known. Come! Let's go!

They all exit.

ACT 5, SCENE 2

Alarum. Enter BRUTUS *and* MESSALA

BRUTUS
Ride, ride, Messala, ride, and give these bills
Unto the legions on the other side.

Low alarum

Let them set on at once, for I perceive
But cold demeanor in Octavius' wing,
And sudden push gives them the overthrow.
Ride, ride, Messala. Let them all come down.

Exeunt severally

ACT 5, SCENE 2

Sounds of battle. BRUTUS *and* MESSALA *enter.*

BRUTUS

Ride, ride, Messala, ride, and give these dispatches to our forces on the other side.

Faint sounds of battle.

They should advance immediately, because I sense Octavius's side is a bit fainthearted right now, and a sudden push would overthrow him. Ride, ride, Messala. Let Cassius's wing mount a surprise attack.

They exit in opposite directions.

ACT 5, SCENE 3

Alarums
Enter CASSIUS *and* TITINIUS

CASSIUS
O, look, Titinius, look, the villains fly!
Myself have to mine own turned enemy.
This ensign here of mine was turning back.
I slew the coward and did take it from him.
(indicates his standard)

TITINIUS
5   O Cassius, Brutus gave the word too early,
Who, having some advantage on Octavius,
Took it too eagerly. His soldiers fell to spoil,
Whilst we by Antony are all enclosed.

Enter PINDARUS

PINDARUS
Fly further off, my lord, fly further off.
10   Mark Antony is in your tents, my lord.
Fly, therefore, noble Cassius, fly far off.

CASSIUS
This hill is far enough.—Look, look, Titinius.
Are those my tents where I perceive the fire?

TITINIUS
They are, my lord.

CASSIUS
                          Titinius, if thou lovest me,
15   Mount thou my horse, and hide thy spurs in him
Till he have brought thee up to yonder troops
And here again, that I may rest assured
Whether yond troops are friend or enemy.

ACT 5, SCENE 3

Sounds of battle. CASSIUS *and* TITINIUS *enter.*

CASSIUS

Oh, look, Titinius, look! Those villains, our soldiers, flee! I've become an enemy to my own soldiers! This standard-bearer here of mine was running away, so I killed him and took the flag from him. *(points to his flag)*

TITINIUS

Oh, Cassius, Brutus gave the orders too soon. Having an advantage over Octavius, he took it too eagerly, and his soldiers began looting, and now we're surrounded by Antony's men.

PINDARUS *enters.*

PINDARUS

Retreat further, my lord, retreat further. Mark Antony is in your tents, my lord. Therefore you must run, noble Cassius.

CASSIUS

This hill is far enough. Look, look, Titinius. Are those my tents on fire?

TITINIUS

They are, my lord.

CASSIUS

Titinius, if you love me, get on your horse and spur him on until he's brought you to those troops and back again, so that I can find out whether those troops are friends or enemies.

TITINIUS
> I will be here again, even with a thought.

Exit TITINIUS

CASSIUS
20   Go, Pindarus, get higher on that hill.
> My sight was ever thick. Regard Titinius,
> And tell me what thou notest about the field.

PINDARUS *ascends the hill*

> This day I breathed first. Time is come round,
> And where I did begin, there shall I end.
25   My life is run his compass.
> *(to* PINDARUS*)*   Sirrah, what news?

PINDARUS
> *(above)* O my lord!

CASSIUS
> What news?

PINDARUS
> *(above)* Titinius is enclosèd round about
> With horsemen, that make to him on the spur.
30   Yet he spurs on. Now they are almost on him.
> Now, Titinius. Now some light. Oh, he lights too.
> He's ta'en.

Shout within

> And, hark! They shout for joy.

CASSIUS
>   Come down, behold no more.
> Oh, coward that I am, to live so long
35   To see my best friend ta'en before my face!

PINDARUS *returns*

TITINIUS

I'll be back quicker than you can think a thought.

He exits.

CASSIUS

Go, Pindarus, climb a little higher on this hill. My eyesight has always been bad. Watch Titinius and tell me what you see in the field.

PINDARUS *ascends the hill.*

Today was the day I breathed my first breath. Time has come round, and I'll end where I began. My life has run its circle. *(to* PINDARUS*)* What can you see, boy?

PINDARUS

(above) Oh, my lord!

CASSIUS

What news?

PINDARUS

(above) Titinius is surrounded by horsemen who are quickly approaching him, yet he spurs onward. Now they're almost on him. Now, Titinius! Now some dismount. Oh, he gets down too. He's taken.

A shout offstage.

And listen! They shout for joy.

CASSIUS

Come down, look no more. Oh, I'm such a coward for living long enough to see my best friend taken before my eyes!

PINDARUS *returns.*

Come hither, sirrah.
In Parthia did I take thee prisoner.
And then I swore thee, saving of thy life,
That whatsoever I did bid thee do,
40   Thou shouldst attempt it. Come now, keep thine oath.
(gives his sword to PINDARUS*)*
Now be a free man, and with this good sword
That ran through Caesar's bowels, search this bosom.
Stand not to answer. Here take thou the hilts
And, when my face is covered, as 'tis now,
45   Guide thou the sword.

PINDARUS *stabs* CASSIUS

                    Caesar, thou art revenged,
Even with the sword that killed thee.
(dies)

PINDARUS
So I am free. Yet would not so have been,
Durst I have done my will. O Cassius,
Far from this country Pindarus shall run,
50   Where never Roman shall take note of him.

                          Exit PINDARUS

Enter TITINIUS *and* MESSALA

MESSALA
It is but change, Titinius, for Octavius
Is overthrown by noble Brutus' power,
As Cassius' legions are by Antony.

TITINIUS
These tidings will well comfort Cassius.

MESSALA
55   Where did you leave him?

Come here, boy. I took you prisoner in Parthia, and at that time I made you swear to try to do whatever I ordered you to, except take your own life. Come now, keep your oath. *(gives his sword to* PINDARUS*)* Now you'll be a free man. Take this good sword, which ran through Caesar's bowels, and plunge it in my chest. Don't hesitate. Here, take the handle, and when my face is covered as it is now, use the sword.

PINDARUS *stabs* CASSIUS.

Caesar, you are revenged with the very same sword that killed you. *(he dies)*

PINDARUS

So I'm free. But I didn't want to be free like this. Oh, Cassius, I'll run far from this country to where no Romans can find me.

He exits.

TITINIUS *and* MESSALA *enter.*

MESSALA

The armies have merely changed places, Titinius, because Octavius has been overthrown by noble Brutus's forces at the very moment that Antony overthrew Cassius's legions.

TITINIUS

This news will comfort Cassius.

MESSALA

Where did you leave him?

TITINIUS
                                    All disconsolate,
With Pindarus his bondman on this hill.

MESSALA
Is not that he that lies upon the ground?

TITINIUS
He lies not like the living. O my heart!

MESSALA
Is not that he?

TITINIUS
                        No, this was he, Messala,
60   But Cassius is no more. O setting sun,
As in thy red rays thou dost sink tonight,
So in his red blood Cassius' day is set.
The sun of Rome is set. Our day is gone.
Clouds, dews, and dangers come! Our deeds are done.
65   Mistrust of my success hath done this deed.

MESSALA
Mistrust of good success hath done this deed.
O hateful error, melancholy's child,
Why dost thou show to the apt thoughts of men
The things that are not? O error, soon conceived,
70   Thou never comest unto a happy birth
But kill'st the mother that engendered thee!

TITINIUS
What, Pindarus! Where art thou, Pindarus?

MESSALA
Seek him, Titinius, whilst I go to meet
The noble Brutus, thrusting this report
75   Into his ears. I may say "thrusting" it,
For piercing steel and darts envenomèd
Shall be as welcome to the ears of Brutus
As tidings of this sight.

TITINIUS

On this hill and in despair, with his slave Pindarus.

MESSALA

Isn't that him on the ground?

TITINIUS

He doesn't seem to be alive. Oh, my heart!

MESSALA

Isn't that him?

TITINIUS

No, it *was* him, Messala, but Cassius is no more. Just as the sun's rays turn red when it sets, so Cassius has ended his life in a pool of red blood. The sun of Rome has set! Our day is over. Clouds, dew, and dangers approach. We're finished! He didn't believe I would ever return on my mission, and so he killed himself.

MESSALA

Yes, he killed himself because he thought we'd lost the whole battle. Sadness, which misconstrues reality, gave birth to his errors in thinking—and then destroyed him.

TITINIUS

Pindarus! Where are you, Pindarus?

MESSALA

Look for him, Titinius, while I go to meet the noble Brutus and force him to hear this news. I say "force" because Brutus would rather I stuck sharp blades and poisoned arrows in his ears than fill them with this.

TITINIUS

Hie you, Messala,
And I will seek for Pindarus the while.

Exit MESSALA

80   Why didst thou send me forth, brave Cassius?
Did I not meet thy friends? And did not they
Put on my brows this wreath of victory
And bid me give it thee? Didst thou not hear their shouts?
Alas, thou hast misconstrued everything!
85   But, hold thee, take this garland on thy brow.
Thy Brutus bid me give it thee, and I
Will do his bidding.
(lays wreath on CASSIUS*'s head)* Brutus, come apace,
And see how I regarded Caius Cassius.
90   —By your leave, gods, this is a Roman's part.
Come, Cassius' sword, and find Titinius' heart.
(stabs himself with CASSIUS*'s sword and dies)*

Alarum. Enter BRUTUS, MESSALA, *young* CATO, STRATO,
VOLUMNIUS, LUCILLIUS, LABIO, *and* FLAVIO

BRUTUS

Where, where, Messala, doth his body lie?

MESSALA

Lo, yonder, and Titinius mourning it.

BRUTUS

Titinius' face is upward.

CATO

He is slain.

BRUTUS

95   O Julius Caesar, thou art mighty yet!
Thy spirit walks abroad and turns our swords
In our own proper entrails.

TITINIUS

Hurry, Messala, and I'll look for Pindarus in the meantime.

MESSALA exits.

Why did you send me out, brave Cassius? Didn't I meet up with your allies? And didn't they place the wreath of victory on my brow and order me to give it to you? Didn't you hear their shouts? Alas, you misunderstood everything! But let me place this wreath on your head. Your Brutus ordered me to give it to you, and I'll do what he says. *(he lays a wreath on CASSIUS's head)* Brutus, come this way and see how much I admired Caius Cassius. With your permission, gods, this is a Roman's duty. Come, Cassius's sword, and strike Titinius's heart. *(he stabs himself with CASSIUS's sword and dies.)*

Sounds of battle. BRUTUS, MESSALA, *young* CATO, STRATO, VOLUMNIUS, LUCILLIUS, LABIO, *and* FLAVIO *enter.*

BRUTUS

Where is his body, Messala?

MESSALA

Over there, where Titinius mourns it.

BRUTUS

Titinius is lying face-up.

CATO

He's been killed.

BRUTUS

Oh, Julius Caesar, you are still powerful. Your ghost walks the earth and turns our swords toward our own stomachs.

Low alarums

CATO
                                        Brave Titinius!—
Look whe 'er he have not crowned dead Cassius.

BRUTUS
Are yet two Romans living such as these?
100   —The last of all the Romans, fare thee well!
It is impossible that ever Rome
Should breed thy fellow.—Friends, I owe more tears
To this dead man than you shall see me pay.
—I shall find time, Cassius, I shall find time.
105   —Come, therefore, and to Thasos send his body.
His funerals shall not be in our camp,
Lest it discomfort us.—Lucillius, come.—
And come, young Cato. Let us to the field.
—Labio and Flavio, set our battles on.
110   —'Tis three o'clock, and, Romans, yet ere night
We shall try fortune in a second fight.

                                        Exeunt

Faint sounds of battle.

CATO

Brave Titinius! Look, he even put the crown on dead
Cassius!

BRUTUS

Could you have found two Romans as good as these
two? Good-bye to you, the last of all the Romans.
Rome will never produce your equal. Friends, I owe
more tears to this dead man than you will see me shed.
I will find the time to cry for you, Cassius, I'll find the
time. Come, then, and send his body to Thasos. We
won't have his funeral at our camp, because it might
make us too sad to fight. Lucillius, come. And come,
young Cato. Let's proceed to the field. Labio and Flavio, push our armies onward. It is three o'clock, and,
Romans, before night, we will try our luck in a second
battle.

They all exit.

ACT 5, SCENE 4

Alarum. Enter BRUTUS, MESSALA, CATO, LUCILLIUS, *and* FLAVIO

BRUTUS
Yet, countrymen, O, yet hold up your heads!

Exeunt BRUTUS, MESSALA, *and* FLAVIO

CATO
What bastard doth not? Who will go with me?
I will proclaim my name about the field.
I am the son of Marcus Cato, ho!
5   A foe to tyrants, and my country's friend.
I am the son of Marcus Cato, ho!

Enter ANTONY *and* OCTAVIUS' SOLDIERS
Fight

LUCILLIUS
And I am Brutus, Marcus Brutus, I!
Brutus, my country's friend. Know me for Brutus!

SOLDIERS *kill young* CATO

O young and noble Cato, art thou down?
10   Why, now thou diest as bravely as Titinius,
And mayst be honored, being Cato's son.

FIRST SOLDIER
(to LUCILLIUS*)* Yield, or thou diest.

LUCILLIUS
                              Only I yield to die.
There is so much that thou wilt kill me straight.
Kill Brutus, and be honored in his death.

ACT 5, SCENE 4

Sounds of battle. BRUTUS, MESSALA, CATO, LUCILLIUS, *and* FLAVIO *enter.*

BRUTUS

Keep on, countrymen. Oh, keep your heads up, even now!

BRUTUS, MESSALA, *and* FLAVIO *exit.*

CATO

Who is so low that he wouldn't? Who will advance with me? I will proclaim my name around the field. I am the son of Marcus Cato! An enemy to tyrants and a friend to my country. I am the son of Marcus Cato!

ANTONY *and* OCTAVIUS' SOLDIERS *enter and fight.*

LUCILLIUS

And I am Brutus, Marcus Brutus. Brutus, my country's friend. Know that I am Brutus!

SOLDIERS *kill young* CATO.

Oh, young and noble Cato, have you been slain? Why, you die now as bravely as Titinius. And you, being Cato's son, will be honored.

FIRST SOLDIER

(to LUCILLIUS*)* Surrender or you will die.

LUCILLIUS

I'd rather die. Here is some money for you to kill me immediately. Kill Brutus and be honored by the killing.

FIRST SOLDIER
15   We must not. A noble prisoner!

Enter ANTONY

SECOND SOLDIER
Room, ho! Tell Antony Brutus is ta'en.

FIRST SOLDIER
I'll tell the news. Here comes the general.
—Brutus is ta'en, Brutus is ta'en, my lord.

ANTONY
Where is he?

LUCILLIUS
20   Safe, Antony. Brutus is safe enough.
I dare assure thee that no enemy
Shall ever take alive the noble Brutus.
The gods defend him from so great a shame!
When you do find him, or alive or dead,
25   He will be found like Brutus, like himself.

ANTONY
(to SOLDIERS*)* This is not Brutus, friend, but, I assure you,
A prize no less in worth. Keep this man safe.
Give him all kindness. I had rather have
Such men my friends than enemies. Go on,
30   And see whether Brutus be alive or dead.
And bring us word unto Octavius' tent
How everything is chanced.

Exeunt severally

FIRST SOLDIER

We must not. He is a noble prisoner!

ANTONY *enters.*

SECOND SOLDIER

Make room! Tell Antony that Brutus has been taken.

FIRST SOLDIER

I'll tell him the news. Oh, here comes the general—
Brutus has been caught, Brutus is taken, my lord.

ANTONY

Where is he?

LUCILLIUS

He's safe, Antony. I can assure you that no enemy will
ever take the noble Brutus alive. The gods protect him
from so great a shame! When you do find him, alive or
dead, he'll be found on his own terms.

ANTONY

(to SOLDIERS*)* This isn't Brutus, friend, but, I assure
you, he is a valuable prize. Keep this man safe. Be
kind to him. I would rather have such men as friends
than enemies. Move on, find out if Brutus is alive or
dead, then return to Octavius's tent to tell us what
you've learned.

They exit in opposite directions.

ACT 5, SCENE 5

Enter BRUTUS, DARDANIUS, CLITUS, STRATO, *and* VOLUMNIUS

BRUTUS

Come, poor remains of friends, rest on this rock.

CLITUS

Statilius showed the torchlight but, my lord,
He came not back. He is or ta'en or slain.

BRUTUS

Sit thee down, Clitus. Slaying is the word.
It is a deed in fashion. Hark thee, Clitus.
(whispers to CLITUS*)*

CLITUS

What, I, my lord? No, not for all the world.

BRUTUS

Peace then! No words.

CLITUS

                                        I'll rather kill myself.

BRUTUS

Hark thee, Dardanius.
(whispers to DARDANIUS*)*

DARDANIUS

                                        Shall I do such a deed?

CLITUS

O Dardanius!

DARDANIUS

O Clitus!

CLITUS

(aside to DARDANIUS*)*
What ill request did Brutus make to thee?

DARDANIUS

(aside to CLITUS*)* To kill him, Clitus. Look, he meditates.

ACT 5, SCENE 5

BRUTUS, DARDANIUS, CLITUS, STRATO, *and* VOLUMNIUS *enter.*

BRUTUS

Come, last of my friends, rest on this rock.

CLITUS

Statilius waved the torchlight at us, but he hasn't come back. He's been captured or killed.

BRUTUS

Sit down, Clitus. Killed, most likely—it's become a trend. Listen, Clitus. *(he whispers to* CLITUS*)*

CLITUS

Who, me, my lord? No, not for all the world.

BRUTUS

Silence, then! Don't give it away.

CLITUS

I'd rather kill myself.

BRUTUS

Listen, Dardanius. *(he whispers to* DARDANIUS*)*

DARDANIUS

Would I dare do something like that?

CLITUS

Oh Dardanius!

DARDANIUS

Oh Clitus!

CLITUS

(speaking so that only DARDANIUS *can hear)* What awful thing did Brutus ask of you?

DARDANIUS

(speaking so that only CLITUS *can hear)* To kill him, Clitus. Look, he's meditating on what to do.

CLITUS

(aside to DARDANIUS*)* Now is that noble vessel full of grief,
That it runs over even at his eyes.

BRUTUS

15   Come hither, good Volumnius. List a word.

VOLUMNIUS

What says my lord?

BRUTUS

Why this, Volumnius:
The ghost of Caesar hath appeared to me
Two several times by night. At Sardis once,
And this last night here in Philippi fields.
20   I know my hour is come.

VOLUMNIUS

Not so, my lord.

BRUTUS

Nay, I am sure it is, Volumnius.
Thou seest the world, Volumnius, how it goes.
Our enemies have beat us to the pit.

Low alarums

It is more worthy to leap in ourselves
25   Than tarry till they push us. Good Volumnius,
Thou know'st that we two went to school together.
Even for that our love of old, I prithee,
Hold thou my sword hilts, whilst I run on it.

VOLUMNIUS

That's not an office for a friend, my lord.

Alarum still

CLITUS

30   Fly, fly, my lord. There is no tarrying here.

CLITUS

(speaking so that only DARDANIUS *can hear)* That noble man is so full of grief that it spills out of his eyes.

BRUTUS

Come here, good Volumnius. Listen a minute.

VOLUMNIUS

What is it, my lord?

BRUTUS

Just this, Volumnius. The ghost of Caesar has appeared to me at night twice. Once at Sardis and once last night, here in Philippi fields. I know that my hour has come.

VOLUMNIUS

No, it hasn't, my lord.

BRUTUS

No, I'm sure it has, Volumnius. You see how the world goes, Volumnius. Our enemies have driven us to the edge of the grave.

Faint sounds of battle.

It's nobler to leap in ourselves than dawdle until they push us. Good Volumnius, you know that we went to school together. For the sake of our old friendship, I ask you, hold my sword handle while I run on it.

VOLUMNIUS

That's not a job for a friend, my lord.

Continued sounds of battle.

CLITUS

Run, run, my lord. We can't wait here.

BRUTUS
Farewell to you.—And you.—And you, Volumnius.
—Strato, thou hast been all this while asleep.
Farewell to thee too, Strato.—Countrymen,
My heart doth joy that yet in all my life
35   I found no man but he was true to me.
I shall have glory by this losing day
More than Octavius and Mark Antony
By this vile conquest shall attain unto.
So fare you well at once, for Brutus' tongue
40   Hath almost ended his life's history.
Night hangs upon mine eyes. My bones would rest,
That have but labored to attain this hour.

Alarum. Cry within "Fly, fly, fly!"

CLITUS
Fly, my lord, fly.

BRUTUS
                Hence. I will follow.

Exeunt CLITUS, DARDANIUS, *and* VOLUMNIUS

I prithee, Strato, stay thou by thy lord.
45   Thou art a fellow of a good respect.
Thy life hath had some smatch of honor in it.
Hold then my sword and turn away thy face
While I do run upon it. Wilt thou, Strato?

STRATO
Give me your hand first.
50   *(holds* BRUTUS' *sword)* Fare you well, my lord.

BRUTUS

Farewell to you, and you, and you, Volumnius. Strato, you've slept this whole time. Farewell to you too, Strato. Countrymen, my heart rejoices that in all my life I knew no men who were untrue to me. I'll have glory in this losing day—more than Octavius and Mark Antony will gain by their foul conquest. So farewell, all, for my tongue has almost finished with its life. I can't see ahead of me. My bones want to rest after helping me up to this hour.

Sounds of battle. Offstage, someone cries, "Run, run, run!"

CLITUS

Run, my lord, run.

BRUTUS

Go on! I'll follow.

CLITUS, DARDANIUS, and VOLUMNIUS exit.

I beg you, Strato, stay by me. You're a man with a good reputation. Your life has had honor in it. Then, hold my sword and turn your face away while I run on it. Will you, Strato?

STRATO

Give me your hand, first. *(holds BRUTUS' sword)* Farewell, my lord.

BRUTUS
> Farewell, good Strato.
> *(runs on his sword)*   Caesar, now be still.
> I killed not thee with half so good a will.
> *(dies)*

> *Alarum. Retreat. Enter* OCTAVIUS, ANTONY, MESSALA,
> LUCILLIUS, *and the army*

OCTAVIUS
> What man is that?

MESSALA
> My master's man.—Strato, where is thy master?

STRATO
55
> Free from the bondage you are in, Messala.
> The conquerors can but make a fire of him.
> For Brutus only overcame himself,
> And no man else hath honor by his death.

LUCILLIUS
> So Brutus should be found.—I thank thee, Brutus,
60
> That thou hast proved Lucillius' saying true.

OCTAVIUS
> All that served Brutus, I will entertain them.
> —Fellow, wilt thou bestow thy time with me?

STRATO
> Ay, if Messala will prefer me to you.

OCTAVIUS
> Do so, good Messala.

MESSALA
>   How died my master, Strato?

STRATO
65
> I held the sword and he did run on it.

MESSALA
> Octavius, then take him to follow thee,
> That did the latest service to my master.

BRUTUS

Farewell, good Strato. *(runs on his sword)* Caesar, you can rest now. I didn't kill you half as willingly. *(he dies)*

Sounds of battle. Trumpets sound a retreat. OCTAVIUS, ANTONY, MESSALA, *and* LUCILLIUS *enter with the army.*

OCTAVIUS

What man is that?

MESSALA

My master's man. Strato, where's your master?

STRATO

Free from the bondage you are in, Messala. The conquerors can only make a fire of him, because only Brutus triumphed over himself, and no other man gets to triumph in his death.

LUCILLIUS

It's fitting that Brutus be found like this. Thank you, Brutus, for proving my prediction true.

OCTAVIUS

I'll take all who served Brutus into my service. You, will you join with me?

STRATO

Yes, if Messala recommends me to you.

OCTAVIUS

Do so, good Messala.

MESSALA

How did my master die, Strato?

STRATO

I held the sword and he ran on it.

MESSALA

Then take this man into your service, Octavius, for he did the final service to my master.

ANTONY
This was the noblest Roman of them all.
All the conspirators save only he
70   Did that they did in envy of great Caesar.
He only in a general honest thought
And common good to all, made one of them.
His life was gentle, and the elements
So mixed in him that Nature might stand up
75   And say to all the world, "This was a man."

OCTAVIUS
According to his virtue let us use him,
With all respect and rites of burial.
Within my tent his bones tonight shall lie
Most like a soldier, ordered honorably.
80   So call the field to rest, and let's away
To part the glories of this happy day.

Exeunt omnes

ANTONY

This was the noblest Roman of them all. All the rest of
the conspirators acted out of jealousy of great Caesar.
Only he acted from honesty and for the general good.
His life was gentle, and the elements mixed so well in
him that Nature might stand up and say to all the
world, "This was a man."

OCTAVIUS

Let's treat him according to his virtue, with all the
respect and rituals of burial. His body will lie in my
tent tonight, with the honorable observance that suits
a soldier. So order the armies to rest, and let's go home
to share the glories of this happy day.

Everyone exits.

SPARKNOTES LITERATURE GUIDES

Notes

Notes

Notes